Every Child a Treasure ...

Joel begins every day full of energy! As soon as he opens his eyes, he has a smile and a look of anticipation on his face. He goes around greeting and hugging everyone (the dog included) as if he hasn't seen them in days and is thrilled to finally be together. What a wonderful way to start a day!

From the Heart:
Stories by Mothers of Children with Special Needs

Authors:
Patricia Bowman (Pat)
Martha Grady (Marti)
Martha Kendrick (Martie)
Jennie Ladew-Duncan
Susan Mentzer (Sue)
Renée Newman
Ruth Pease
Kathleen Son (Kathy)
Lynn Spadinger

Editors:
Jayne D.B. Marsh, Editor
Carol Boggis, Consulting Editor

Project Staff:
Susan E. Partridge, L.C.S.W., Ph.D., Principal Investigator
John Hornstein, M.Ed., Project Director
Susan B. Soule, L.C.S.W., Project Coordinator
Jayne D. B. Marsh, M.S.N., M.P.A., Research Associate
Deborah Devine, Psy.D., Research Associate

Parents in Partnership Project
Edmund S. Muskie Institute of Public Affairs
University of Southern Maine
Portland, Maine
April, 1994

Published in the United States by the Edmund S. Muskie Institute of Public Affairs, University of Southern Maine, 96 Falmouth Street, Portland, Maine 04103. Funded in part by the U.S. Maternal and Child Health Bureau of the Department of Health and Human Services (Project # MCJ235068).

Copyright© 1994 by the University of Southern Maine
All rights reserved, including the right of reproduction in whole or in part in any form.

Library of Congress Cataloging in Publication Data

Bowman, Patricia, Martha Grady, Martha Kendrick, Jennie Ladew-Duncan, Susan Mentzer, Renée Newman, Ruth Pease, Kathleen Son, Lynn Spadinger
From the Heart: Stories by Mothers of Children with Special Needs
1. Children with Special Needs 2. Special Needs 3. Mothers of Children with Special Needs

Book and cover design by Anne Bernard

Additional copies available from:
  Edmund S. Muskie Institute of Public Affairs
  University of Southern Maine
  96 Falmouth Street
  Portland, Maine 04103
  (207) 780-4430

My son is four today.
Towheaded and gray-eyed, he is all
beaming smiles, sly grins and dancing eyes.
Dashing, leaping, darting, he exhausts each day.
Quicksilver. Four years wise.
Happy, healthy. Alive.

Four years ago today, sickening suspicion became fear.
Became dread, pain, panic.
Too soon, too small, this baby, my baby, whose movements were
still so faint, ephemeral, was to be born.
Fifteen weeks early.
The odds incomprehensible: ten percent survive.

Dogged and brave, he was born,
one and one half pounds of pure soul and will.
At once frail, impossibly fragile, yet indomitable.
Swaddled in a great technological womb, time stopped.
We waited, watched. Exulted and despaired.
Impotent.

Four years is a lifetime to a boy: vast and unfathomable.
Four months an eternity to his mother. An eternity of
days measured by breaths per minute and oxygen levels,
by breast milk in drops and weight in grams.
Diapers weighed and recorded.
Infinitesimal triumphs and terrifying setbacks.

My son, my son. The universe lay with him,
incubated and intubated. So far from home.
Cracks in the armor hastily constructed, widened as
hours became days, became weeks, then months.
Asleep, I searched at midnight through the hamper
for my missing baby. Grieving, exhausted.

Four years later, the scars that so thwarted those tiny lungs,
are insignificant to those of a four-year-old.
Needle scars only tiny marks on his hands and feet.
And so I hope those first months too have paled to insignificance,
the psychic scars shrinking until there is no trace,
no memory. No ghosts.

Leave the ghosts to mother.
My son is four today.

Ruth

Table of Contents

Acknowledgements *Jayne D.B. Marsh*	v
Foreword *Dr. Robert Marion*	ix
Being Heard	1
Feeling Understood	33
Life Amplified	49
Chronicity	81
Coping	103
Healing	125
Afterword *Susan Partridge*	139
About the Authors	143
About Project PIP	147
Key Words	149

Acknowledgements

The idea for this book came out of the support group process established by the Parents in Partnership (PIP) Project for mothers of children with special needs. Every group meeting began with each mother sharing current thoughts on family, work or other important issues. The storytelling that resulted was truly touching, and strong support developed from this exercise.

The mothers and staff of the project wanted to share these stories with other parents, to extend the parent group process and offer something to parents after the project ended. All the mothers felt that hearing stories of other mothers in similar situations was very affirming, and offered them support and strength in dealing with their own issues. They felt less alone.

My strongest feelings around my child with special needs are first inadequacy and then fear.

Martie

We offer this book as a testament to all families of children with special needs. These families are faced with endless daily challenges of an intensity far beyond what is "normal" for most parents. The effort needed is time-consuming and sometimes overwhelming. The responsibility is unending, and support is not always available. The constant emotional roller coaster impacts all other aspects of life. The highs are very emotional, and the lows extremely frustrating. The stories included display this intensity, both the pain *and* the joy.

> *Listen, just listen. That is my biggest fear — people won't listen.*
>
> *Kathy*

The stories included in this book are grouped in chapters or sections according to the theme they convey, themes that came out of many discussions with the authors during the group process. The first themes focus primarily on relationships with professionals. The middle sections deal with family life and school issues. The last sections deal with very personal feelings and issues about the "self" and those to whom the authors are closest.

The stories either were told in a support group setting and transcribed/edited later, or were written as reflective thoughts of various lived experiences. "Words of Wisdom" (W.O.W.!) by the authors are also found in the margins throughout the book. These statements stood out from reflective, introspective moments or were spontaneous representations of an individual's feelings or emotions at a given moment during the group process. They and the stories were collected for this book to help validate and comfort other parents and provide special insight to both parents and professionals into what life is like for parents of children with special needs.

> The overwhelming emotion I felt when Joel was born was fear, fear of the unknown. What else is lurking around the corner? Can I handle this? Can I cope? Can I be a good mother to this child? Can I balance the needs of my other two children? Can our marriage survive this?
>
> *Lynn*

The staff would like to thank the mothers involved with us on this project. Their openness and honesty in telling their stories has provided much to us (professionally and personally) to the project, and to all those involved with or impacted by the project.

We would also like to acknowledge the work of Anne Bernard, whose expertise and creativity in computer graphics show in the design of the book. Carol Boggis lent her comprehensive editing skills towards a polished final project. Evelyn St. Pierre and Paula Mulherin, our administrative assistants, came through as always, with their energy and optimism which kept us moving forward.

Dr. Robert Marion has been a friend to the project, offering his knowledge and expertise to us on many occasions. His support was very affirming, as was his willingness to take part in our product development.

Project PIP, in its three years, endeavored to support parents of children with special needs and enlighten the professionals they rely on about the need for establishing partnerships. As the project ends, it is our hope that the notion of partnerships between parents and professionals will become more than a notion–a lasting reality.

Project PIP offers this book to other parents of children with special needs in the hope that it provides something to each parent who reads it. We additionally hope that professionals will find it valuable in increasing their understanding of parents of children with special needs. *Together* we can work more effectively than if we move along separate paths.

> Jayne D. B. Marsh
> Editor

Foreword

What Doctors Think Patients Want from Their Doctors
by Dr. Robert Marion

"What do my patients want from me? Not much really... just all my time, my blood, my sweat, my brain, my heart, and maybe my first-born child. That's all."
A pediatrician in private practice,
Westchester County, New York

It's so simple that busy practicing physicians don't tend to give the question even a passing thought. After four years of medical school, a year of internship, two or more years of residency, and possibly two or three years of fellowship training, it seems so obvious that we all know exactly what our patients want, what we believe they've come to expect from us, that it's not even worthy of consideration anymore. It's a lesson we learn starting on the very first day of medical school: unquestionably, patients want their doctors to make a quick and accurate diagnosis, come up with a suitable treatment plan (preferably one that doesn't hurt or cause too much inconvenience), and, in no time at all, cure their patient's medical problems.

But where does this information come from? Are actual patients invited to medical school orientation, or to residency training sessions, to express their views? Do trainees go onto the wards or units of the hospital soliciting answers to this most vital question from people who are ill? Are pollsters hired to survey a segment of consumers? Of course not. The answer is provided for us by our teachers; physicians who have chosen to devote their lives to teaching new doctors in addition to caring for patients. And where did our teachers learn this lesson? It was passed on to them by their teachers, of course.

After some consideration, it has become clear that a problem exists here. Somehow, in the training of physicians, an important component has been eliminated from the loop: patients are never asked what it is, exactly, that they want. It's always only assumed that the lesson that's taught is correct. But after all, what else is it that a patient in his right mind could want?

As a pediatric geneticist, I came to realize early in my career that the formula that was outlined during medical school wasn't exactly going to work for me. In only about half of the children with congenital malformations I follow will a definitive diagnosis be made; and in virtually no cases will a suitable treatment plan that leads to a cure be possible. So I've had to make adjustments; I've learned that there are other therapies I could offer my patients, treatments that might substitute for my inability to offer a magic bullet that will allow life to return to normal.

Madeline D. stopped by my office last week. She had some forms that needed to be filled out for Aisha's home care agency and, using this as a premise, dropped by to talk.

I've known Madeline now for more than ten years. In 1982, she was referred for evaluation to the genetics center at which I was doing my fellowship training. At 40 years of age and with out-of-control diabetes mellitus, she and I both knew that the fetus she was then carrying was in danger of being affected with a multitude of serious problems. But during our initial counseling session, Madeline expressed how greatly she wanted this baby: with three grown children, all but the youngest of them already out of the house, this pregnancy represented, in her mind, her last chance to feel young and alive.

We did what we could to monitor Madeline's pregnancy: I was with her when an amniocentesis was performed at sixteen weeks gestation and, three weeks later, had the pleasure of informing her that the fetus had a normal female chromosome complement; I was with her when three separate sonograms were done, and, following each study, was glad to be able to report that no abnormalities had been detected; and I was there when, at 32 weeks gestation, she fell into premature labor and delivered a critically ill infant.

Aisha, as the baby was named, was sick from the very beginning. Her prematurity led to severe respiratory distress syndrome, a condition that required ventilator support for weeks. But Aisha's problems weren't limited to those that re-

sulted from having been born eight weeks too soon: at birth, multiple congenital defects, anomalies that had failed to be detected by the serial sonograms we'd performed, were identified. The infant had a malformed left ear and eye, part of a condition known as hemifacial microsomia; she had a defective vertebral body in the upper portion of her spine, a condition that led to scoliosis, or curvature of the spine; she had a double collecting system of her right kidney; and, most importantly, she had a series of holes in the ventricular septum, the wall that separates the left and right pumping chambers of the heart. Grateful that the infant was alive but scared to death concerning what the future might hold, Madeline seemed paralyzed; all we could do to support her during those early days was to keep assuring her that everything possible was being done to keep Aisha going.

The infant progressed well and left the hospital at three months of age. Follow-up was arranged with her regular pediatrician, as well as a nephrologist, a pulmonologist, an orthopedic surgeon, a cardiologist, and with me. During the yearly visits she made to my office, I took pleasure in watching how well she and her mother were doing: while Aisha grew and developed, Madeline took immense pride in her daughter. The interactions between them made me feel good, cheering me up during some otherwise fairly depressing days of office hours.

But when Aisha was six, events took a dramatic turn. The first sign that something was wrong occurred early in the school year: Aisha, usually a bundle of energy, began taking long naps after returning from first grade. Believing at first it was nothing more than an adjustment to the longer hours of first grade, Madeline didn't make much of her daughter's drowsiness, not even calling it to the attention of any of Aisha's doctors. But then Aisha had a planned, initial appointment at our craniofacial center, the facility that was going to coordinate the plastic surgical repair of the little girl's malformed ear. It was during that appointment that Aisha's and Madeline's lives started coming apart.

The pediatrician who examined Aisha that day at the craniofacial center noticed the girl's pallor and the blue-tinged discoloration around her lips and fingertips. While listening with his stethoscope, he heard a loud murmur in the little girl's chest. Although Madeline informed him that, after two years of follow-up in the cardiology clinic, the murmur had disappeared and the child had been discharged, judged to be cured of her congenital heart defect, the pediatrician knew something was wrong. He sent her off for an immediate echocardiogram.

In piecing the story together now, it's difficult to know for sure exactly who was to blame, but assessing blame was not all that important. Clearly, some error occurred during that last cardiology visit, for Aisha's heart defect had never disappeared. The echocardiogram showed that the holes in the ventricular septum were still present. And these holes had led to a condition called Eisenmenger's Complex, a disorder in which the walls of the small blood vessels in the lungs grow so thick that carbon dioxide and oxygen can no longer pass through them— a lethal, untreatable condition. Aisha, so loved and cherished by her parents, was doomed to die a slow, uncomfortable death because of what amounted to nothing more than human error.

In the years that have passed since the discovery was made, as we've unsuccessfully tried every avenue possible to reverse Aisha's apparently terminal condition, Madeline and I have had numerous conversations. Pulling no punches, keeping nothing from her, I've told her exactly what happened, when it happened, and, to the best of my knowledge, how it happened. She fully understands that her daughter is dying, has watched her weaken and worsen so that now the child, who underwent a tracheostomy last year, requires ventilatory support at night; and she knows that nothing can be done to reverse the inevitable. We've talked about Aisha's funeral, about where she'll be buried, and, only recently, what life will be like for Madeline after she's gone. Other than giving her a flu shot, checking her heart and lungs, and treating her infections, there's nothing I can do to help Aisha.

There is, however, a great deal I can do for Madeline. Although I've gotten her into regular counseling with a psychologist, she still comes to my office regularly, just to talk. So last week, with Aisha's home care forms in hand, she sat down on my couch and started to talk.

Even before she started, I could see she was very upset: her eyes were clouded and her shoulders slumped. "I'm getting so tired of this, Dr. Marion," she began. "None of them (her family) cares about anything but themselves. I don't know how much longer I can take it."

When I asked her what she meant, Madeline continued: "I do everything any of them needs. I spend my life caring for Aisha. Rocky [her husband] is of no help at all. And when one of my older kids needs something, it's, 'Mom can you get this?' or, 'Mom, can you do that?' I just bought my daughter a new ice box with the money I was going to use to buy myself a CD player. I'm still helping my son pay off his pickup truck. And do I get any thanks? Of course not..."

Madeline talked for a good twenty-five minutes. As she talked, I could see that she was unloading the burden she'd carried into my office. Her eyes cleared and started to sparkle again, like they did in the days before Aisha first went to the craniofacial center. Her shoulders raised and she held her head up again. It was as if she had been transformed.

And although "transformed" may be too strong a word, perhaps it's better to describe Madeline as energized. She didn't need me to say anything; she didn't need me to cure her daughter (although, clearly, she would have loved that); all she needed was to have someone to talk to, or, more accurately, to talk at, someone who wouldn't criticize her, or answer her back, or feel guilty. And when she was finished, after she'd been unburdened, she was ready to head back into the fray that was her life, at least for a while. Unburdener: That's the role I've come to play with Madeline D.

Unburdener is a role I've come to play with a lot of families. I'd led myself to believe that if you listen carefully enough, almost every patient and family member will tell you right up front what it is he or she needs from you. Some do, in fact, come in requiring a prescription for that elusive magic bullet; unfortunately, these people often leave very disappointed. Some need a listener, an unburdener, like Madeline D.; some need a counselor; others need an advisor, a person with medical knowledge off of whom they can bounce ideas about their child's well-being.

So, naively, I'd come to believe that I'd taken the lesson I learned in medical school about what patients need, a step further. I knew there was more to medicine than diagnosis and cure, and I have to say, up until recently, I was pretty damned satisfied with myself.

And then I became involved with Parents In Partnership (PIP).

It was while working with PIP that I saw the fault in my logic. Yes, there was more to medicine than diagnosis, treatment, and cure, but I hadn't found the answer: like the people who taught me, I'd assumed I knew something that I didn't really know. Like my teachers, I had never bothered actually asking my patients what it was they wanted from me.

While attending an organizational meeting in Portland, I realized that there was more here than I originally thought. And the first time I watched the videotape PIP produced, *Every Child a Treasure*, my mouth nearly dropped open: I became convinced that neither I nor any of my colleagues in medicine, no matter how tuned in or attentive we believed ourselves to be, had even an inkling concerning what our patients viewed as important.

And in much the same way that *Every Child a Treasure* opened my eyes, the stories that follow will open readers' hearts. Touching and sincere, filled with the unsweetened, unadulterated emotions of parents of children with special needs, these stories chronicle the struggles and successes, the happy endings and the setbacks, the failures and accomplishments that occur virtually every day in the lives of families trying their best to raise a child who is different in one way or another from what's considered normal. Read these stories slowly; savor them and think about them. They can and will change the way you think about life.

Dr. Robert Marion is a pediatric geneticist at Montefiore Hospital in the Bronx, New York and Associate Professor at the Albert Einstein College of Medicine.

In the essential sadness of all of this is the Glory.
Everything that is wonderful about that child,
all of the love and devotion I feel for my child.
It is not separate from the sadness,
it isn't just the badness.
It is painful joy,
or joyful pain,
the two are together.

Kathy

Being Heard...

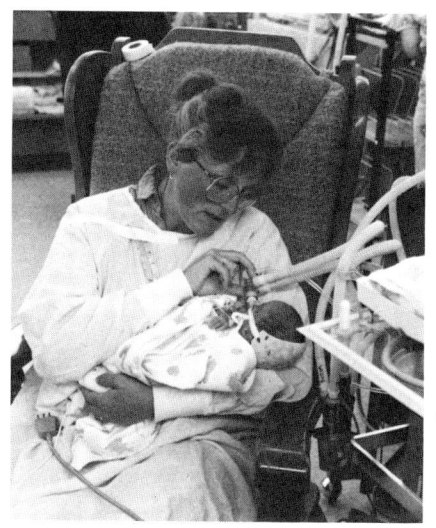

For parents of children with special needs, being heard is one of the most important aspects of their relationships with others. Being heard by their family members, both immediate and extended; friends, neighbors, community members and/or work associates; and especially the professional providers upon whom they rely for help and guidance. These parents need others to listen to their concerns and feelings. Many are grieving over their child's condition. It doesn't matter where they are in this process; what matters is their need to be heard.

The stories that follow reflect this need, and the impact it has on the lives of these families, from the mothers' own perspectives.

We all have an innate need to be heard, to be validated, to feel okay about what we have to say. Again and again this comes up: in our marriages, in our relationships with family and friends, and in our relationships with professionals. What we have to say is valid and valuable. The professionals we deal with need to realize that. We could all benefit from listening to others more carefully in our everyday life.

I once wrote a letter to my sister in an attempt to work through the tension in our relationship resulting from my having a child with special needs. My hope was that she would hear me and understand. I want to share that letter.

> *Driving home from your house today, the vision of you standing in your driveway has remained with me. Hands on your hips, slight frown furrowing your brow, you are every inch my big sister.*
>
> *I know that I have displeased you, Lori. My crying about Laura's diagnosis seemed somehow to disgust you. I am writing this letter in the hope that once you read it, you will try to overcome your revulsion to my pain and perhaps even try to help me bear it. I have this awful doomy kind of feeling that I'm in for some difficult years ahead.*
>
> *What you said didn't help, you know; your snappy, "Look, Kathy, you've just got to learn to accept this" stunned me. Accept it? I wanted to scream, **accept it**? I'll never accept this, never ever accept that my baby has cerebral palsy, is "developmentally delayed" (Whatever that means! Why don't they say "retarded" any more?) or might never walk or talk. It's just not acceptable to me that she will*

have pain, be "different" (Isn't the word "special" these days?), and may have a reduced life span. No, no, no...It's no more acceptable to me that it's my baby than if, God forbid, it were yours.

That my marriage might crumble under "the stress" or that we might go broke from all the medical bills or that Dustin might always feel he's second in importance to us are possibilities that haunt me daily. God, I'm so scared. I keep thinking that maybe, just maybe, none of this is true or that tomorrow I'll wake up and this will all be some awful nightmare, but I think not. My one hope right now is that I can somehow make it through all this without losing my sanity... or my sister.

I need you, Lori. I need you to just let me cry if I need to and still accept me. I need you to just hear me out without fearing that my feelings will put you off. I need your support right now _ more than I've ever needed it, I need it now.

I'm thinking that this letter could make or break our relationship, Lori, but that's a risk I have to take. If I can't be me, well, then, I've lost more than I even thought I had.

Being heard is the single most important idea. Every time I had a conflict, it was about being heard, in varying degrees. Jeremy had cancer and no one would listen to me saying that this kid was sick. I went here, I went there, we took him to the hospital, we were told, "There's nothing to worry about." The surgeon sent a note to the pediatrician that said, "This child doesn't have cancer." So this specialist told us to take Jeremy home. I took him back to the pediatrician and I pleaded with her until she heard me. To this day I thank God that that woman listened to me. I said, "I'm going crazy. I am losing it. They don't want to operate. If they don't do it, I'm going to go off the deep end."

I was never so close in my life, out of all these experiences, to going off the deep end. The pediatrician called the pediatric surgeon and convinced him that I was going to go crazy if they didn't do something, and that's what got him to do the surgery. It was such an exasperating, draining experience. A biopsy was all I wanted! If the pediatrician hadn't listened to me, things would not have happened the way they did. The cancer wouldn't have been found in time, the chemotherapy wouldn't have worked, and Jeremy wouldn't be here. What it boils down to is an instinct.

In the middle of surgery Jeremy was in a holding pattern, and the surgeon came down and said to me, "You know, I didn't think it would take so long, but I have to tell you, he has cancer." And he looked at me and said, "You're not surprised." I said, "No, I knew I was fighting something stronger than mother love itself." I knew that was it. I mean I had told other people this. Now I said, "I know what I can do. Now there is a plan." Finally I was heard, then we could go forward, because we had found the problem. For me, that was it, just being heard.

Being heard is important in every aspect of your life.

Lynn

We want to be heard. We want them to listen. But what professionals often hear, and what I think we sometimes imply, is that we want them to "fix it," and when they can't and they don't have any control over that, they start blaming us. They get frustrated and angry. I run into the same thing in my marriage. My husband cannot listen to me when I tell him what's happening at work, because what he hears is that he needs to fix it, and when he can't fix it, he thinks, "What's the point of listening?" You translate that into a professional relationship with someone who doesn't have the same level of caring for you and they distance. That's their way of dealing with it. They don't, they won't, or they blame; they turn it around on you.

One of the things that's different about women is that we need to share our feelings. It's such a sense of loneliness when you're dealing with this, and you need to share that with someone. And that's what's hard on the marriage, because men aren't like that. They don't understand that we just need to share that; they feel that we want them to make it better. I've experienced this with my husband. I say, "I'm not wanting you to fix this. I know you can't make this better, but please just hear what I'm telling you." It's an awful burden to have on my own shoulders. Sometimes that's how I feel, alone.

It's being believed, just that. That is the essence of it for me, that it's really like this, that I'm not just making it up. What matters is trust. This is what matters most in my relationship with professionals. With my individual therapist, I have that trust, I know that she trusts me. She knows that I'm telling the truth. We've built this relationship where I don't need to say, "No, really, honest to God, this happened..." I can just start talking and we get to where I really am. I experience that as trust, that I am not a nut case, that what I say is worthy of being regarded.

This struggle to be heard, to be validated, is never ending. My husband and I have been going to marriage counseling around the issues of having a child with special needs. As I was sitting with this professional and my husband talking about all these issues – the emotions, how constant the struggle is, doing it alone – the therapist stopped me and said, "This would be a good time for us to really look at something here. Don't mind that I've interrupted, but what I think is that down the road we are going to need to look at getting you, Kathy, evaluated for manic depression. A little medication," he said, "will make you feel better, more able to sleep, and you'll be able to deal with your husband more happily."

I just sat there, and I thought, this is it, I'm not being heard, and now it's so bad that I have to be shut up. I have to be medicated. He's going to medicate me. This is insane. There's something absurd about my being labeled "sick" because I shared my feelings, my pain. It's almost as if what I said was so painful to hear that the therapist needed to shut me up so he wouldn't have to deal with it. It brought back to me how we become the problem because we are willing to talk about the way it *really* is. And I scream out, "Does anybody really get it?" Whether it's teachers or professionals, there are times when I think we have a really hard time being acknowledged or respected, and our perspectives validated.

I once had an incident where I was trying to tell a professional the bizarre things that Laura was doing, and they said, "But isn't she pretty?" I kept trying to say, "This is awful," and they'd say, "Isn't she cute?" I was feeling misunderstood, invalidated and minimized. All of us, including physicians, nurses, teachers, OT's, PT's, etcetera, have had these experiences where we've felt this way. Isn't there some way for professionals to develop an understanding of the issues for parents of children with special needs, that taps into some of their own life experiences?

Matthew has a meeting next week at school during which we will talk to various school personnel about how to make his program happen. This will be interesting because I'm working with someone in the school who is a learning strategist, but just doesn't understand what a learning disability attention deficit disorder (ADD) is. She thinks Matthew ought to be able to take a computer into middle school, to three different classes, and be responsible in a hallway with lots of people, and, in three minutes time, run his papers around during lunch time, handing them in to his various teachers. He can barely remember to put his papers in his backpack in the morning, let alone give them to his teachers, but the learning strategist doesn't hear me when I tell her this. And if she can't hear me, she can't understand what it's like for Matthew, or for me.

They have a "life-space" room at Asher's school. That's where the children who are acting out are isolated while they think about and, eventually, discuss their aberrant behaviors. I told his teacher that Asher would consider this approach aversive, that he responds better to positive reinforcement. There's not much that Asher likes, but he's really enthused (i.e., obsessed) with cars. When his teacher "discovered" that the "life-space" room wasn't working, she found that the incentive, or positive reinforcement, of a trip to the local car dealership worked wonders as a behavior modification. Asher now has a stack of new car brochures nearly as tall as he is. He even calls the 800 numbers and requests videos and information. We get calls from local Jaguar dealerships wanting to know when "Mr. Kendrick" is planning to purchase his next Jaguar!

My parents were here for about five days, and it was a good visit. My parents have been around Jess before, but it had been a year and a half since they saw her last. So, when we've talked on the phone, they didn't really understand. I think that they thought I was blowing things out of proportion, or that Jess was not able to speak because my parenting had somehow created less incentive for her to want to speak. As time goes on, and they see that she is just not outgrowing her differences, they are realizing their granddaughter has disabilities.

When my parents were here, I gave them a recent developmental assessment about Jessica that had evaluations from about seven different health care and educational professionals – you know, the "experts." They read the assessment and realized that Jess has "real" problems. It's really too bad that a mother's knowledge about her child is minimized and invalidated, even by her own family, unless supported by the "experts."

I often hear people comment on how happy kids with Down syndrome are and how loving. Then why are we having so much trouble with Joel hitting and throwing tantrums right now? That image of "dumb and happy" is so unfair. Joel is a typical child; sometimes he's happy and loving and sometimes he's downright miserable. Sometimes he's friendly and charming, and sometimes he's a brat.

It's validation that we're not nuts, that we're dealing with it the best we can and someone out there hears us...

> *They may or may not understand, but you're not losing it. And when you are just about ready to lose it, that's what helps you.*
>
> *Sue*

Sounds like a typical six-year-old, doesn't it?

I remember a time when Robby had this little accident while he was riding his tricycle outside. He hit a bump at the end of the sidewalk, flipped over it and knocked a tooth out, root and all. It was about six o'clock at night, and my regular dentist's phone didn't have a message about what to do in an emergency. So we called and found a dentist who was open, and this dentist thought it would be nice to try and put the tooth back in and see if we could save it. So we spent the next two and a half hours trying to shove this tooth back in. This is with a child whose mouth has already been traumatized. The dentist did not give him anything for the pain (not that I actually wanted him to), but the fact that they expected Robby to sit there and let them push this tooth back in was pretty bad.

The next day the tooth started to come out, so we went to a pediatric dentist who said, "I don't care about his tooth, I think his jaw is broken." I started hyperventilating at this. The pediatric dentist called an oral surgeon and we went right over. The oral surgeon wanted to get a full mouth x-ray and I thought, "This is just silly. You can't get this kid to stand still while this machine goes around him." But there was this wonderful nurse who convinced him that he was driving a train and we got a perfect x-ray. His jaw was fine, not even cracked, there was nothing wrong with it.

But we still had this tooth that had bonded to the other teeth after having slid down. Robby wouldn't even open his mouth by then, which nobody blamed him for, but we made an appointment and went back the next day. They put him to sleep for two minutes, yanked that tooth out, manipulated his jaw, and made sure the other teeth weren't loose or cracked. Everybody I talked to, except the dentist we saw the night the tooth came out, said, "Why did anyone try to put that tooth back in?" Not one of at least a half a dozen other people felt the tooth should have been put back in. This was a baby tooth and they said baby teeth never bond back in properly.

Accepting how we feel about things is also very important. Our feelings are not right or wrong, they are simply real.

Lynn

I had felt sort of angry that when we left the dentist's office the first night with this child, who had screamed and cried until his mouth was numb from being traumatized, the dentist said we shouldn't use that tooth for three weeks! I thought, "Why don't we just take it back out now?" I knew something was really weird. We obviously picked the wrong person to call that night.

I talked to our pediatrician about this situation before Robby had the two minutes of gas, because I wanted to touch base with him. He put this all in perspective for me and really made me feel much better about it. I was feeling really guilty. He was real quiet and chuckled a little, then he said, "Isn't it great that he can be out there riding a bike and have a kid accident? And he's going to have more of them." He made me sit back and think, and it really did make me feel better. He's right, I should be glad this doctor visit wasn't because he needed oxygen or because of something that had to do with his health, it was a kid-type accident. His comment helped me put it all into perspective.

My son Matt is going to middle school next year, so I started to activate the process to change schools, to transition him. I was told by our learning strategist and everybody else that we had to make an appointment with the principal. So I called the office and asked to make the appointment with the principal, and I was told they don't do that. They said that I had to go through the guidance office, so they switched me to the guidance office. I told them that my son would be coming there next year and I wanted to make an appointment with the principal. The guidance office told me they couldn't do that until I talked with a guidance counselor, so a little later a woman called me and asked why on earth would I want to talk to the principal and what was the problem. I tried to explain to her that my son would be coming there next year and that he was a rather unique child, that he has attention deficit hyperactivity disorder (ADHD), learning disorder (LD), and is gifted.

I have a friend whose son went there this year and he had previously been totally mainstreamed. The middle school put him in a resource room as the primary classroom, without talking to the parents or telling them beforehand that this was where he spent his time. It is because I really don't want this to happen to my son that I called the school.

I tried to explain to this guidance counselor how difficult things are for him and that he needs a computer in the classroom. Her response was that the transition team would decide that. She asked if this was in his Individualized Education Program (IEP) and I said, "Yes, it is, that he needs a computer in the classroom. He is totally mainstreamed with a computer. He has attention deficit and it is very difficult for him to make transitions of any kind." She said, "Well, we do a wonderful job of transitioning all the students, this is what we do, and I'm sure he will be just fine. Why do you really think you want to talk to the principal?" "I want to talk to him about the type of student he is getting next year," I said. She said, "Well, I really don't think that's necessary." "Well then," I said, "I'd like to at least come in and observe the classrooms." She answered, "Well, I don't know if I can arrange it. We'll see if I can arrange it. Call me back in March." I said, "Well, listen, this is really important to me. He cannot communicate to me what is going on. He cannot sit long enough to focus on his thoughts and come home and explain to me the way that the middle school is operating. So, if I don't come in and see for myself, (1) I am not going to know how to help him transition and (2) I'm not going to know what he's going through next fall."

"Well, call me back the first week of March and we'll talk about it," she insisted. So I got off the phone and thought, "My gosh, that lady must have thought she handled me really well." She didn't hear me, she didn't hear a thing I said to her, and that really bothered me.

So I started over. I called the school again and I said, "I want to speak to the principal." I got the principal and I said, "I would like to have a meeting with you." So I go in this Friday. It's just an example of how we are handled. The guidance counselor just wasn't listening at all to anything I was saying: the fact that what my son has is debilitating enough to make him non-functional in the regular classroom, that he has to see psychiatrists, talk to counselors, work as a team; and this is her way of trying to help him prepare? So *I* decided what he needed and just did it without her.

Yesterday we had a doctor's appointment. This was a nine o'clock appointment with a pediatric specialist in town. We were there at five minutes to nine. I had to take Jeremy out of school to be there. He was there for ADHD (we are trying to pursue this), and we waited and waited and waited. It got to be

9:15, and the next patient came in and said, "I'm here to see Dr. So-and-So, my appointment is for 9:15." Two minutes later the doctor came out and took him in and there we were, still sitting, waiting.

I went up to the receptionist and I said, "My appointment was at nine o'clock, I'm very angry about this. I have a son I had to take out of school to be here, and we had to sit and wait. He's a child, it's very hard on him and it's very hard on me." Jeremy is not the most cooperative child in the world, and in the next five to ten minutes he was sitting there screaming, "My turn, my turn, my turn." And I felt like, "Come on Jeremy, keep it up, this is great!" What could I do? It's not like the doctor could leave that patient. But I was very, very mad. The receptionist kind of looked at me every so often and I just glared at her.

After we'd had 15 or 20 minutes of extra waiting, the doctor came back out and called Jeremy. We'd been there almost an hour. We had the first appointment of the day and we were there almost an hour before we even saw the doctor. I went in and said, "Before we get started, I have to talk to you about something. We were here for a nine o'clock appointment, and we were here on time. I have a child that I took out of school to be here. I made a nine o'clock appointment so we wouldn't have to wait and we waited anyway. It's terrible when you see the person coming in behind you go in first. Whoever made this mistake ought to be spoken with about this. This is a child we are talking about, a child who is here for ADHD. He does not do well in a waiting room." He said, "Well, I made the mistake. I was running slow and I didn't read who was first."

This guy is a pediatric specialist. Why can't he be sensitive to these issues? My son was there for hyperactivity. We were there *because* he can't sit still and cooperate. It just sometimes makes me feel like I'm banging my head against a wall. The thing was the doctor – he didn't become defensive, but he didn't like me talking to him like that and he didn't like hearing it at all. He was very nervous with me talking to him and telling him these things, but I thought, this is his practice, he ought to know and be aware of this and be sensitive to these issues.

I said to him, "If you're going to be working with me and we're going to work together to figure this out for him, then you need to hear how I feel about this." That's how I prefaced it when I started. I felt good and I don't have a problem working with this doctor now, but...it just doesn't ever cease. Sometimes you think, "Why does this always happen to me?" But I know darn well that there are other parents out there who this happens to every day, and 99.9 percent say nothing. At least I know that maybe the next time, this particular doctor will be a little more aware, and a little more sensitive to the person who's sitting out there with a child, waiting...

Laura is seven and a half now, and we have been discovering new diagnoses for six of those years. At about the time my daughter was four or five months old, I began to have a gnawing sense that something just wasn't quite right with her. Maybe it was because I'm a nurse; maybe I was comparing her to her older brother; maybe, even, it was a mother's instinct; but something told me Laura was not "normal," that the healthy robust infant we'd brought home from the hospital was developing quite abnormally right before my eyes.

Part of what troubled me was the way Laura would arch her back and posture her arms during feeding times or cuddling. Touch seemed intolerable to her. She cried incessantly – shrill, ear-piercing screeches that not only frustrated but genuinely alarmed me – and I constantly wondered, how could a baby cry so long and so hard and still *survive*?

I told Laura's pediatrician of my concern and thankfully he heard me out. But interestingly, his feedback seemed to be limited to comments about my inability to cope. "Oh, Kathy," he would say, "You're just spoiled because your son was an easy baby," and, "Sure, the second one is harder, there's twice as much work." I felt that *I* had the problem, I was evidently a lightweight, a bad sport. And, truthfully, his observations harkened back to me very similar comments I'd made to patients years earlier when I was charge nurse on a surgical unit. When patients would confide to me, "I'm afraid I'm never going to walk again," I couldn't deal with the rawness of their pain, the complexity of their issues, and the time that would be needed for me to help them sort these issues out. So, I'd get light, I'd get glib: "Oh, Mr. Smith, you're just gloomy because it's rainy" or "snowy" or "windy" or "winter." I'd say whatever I needed to say to be off the hook, away from the pain, out of that room.

> *Why do we have to be so separate? Why can't we say "We"? Why say, "We're this, you're that"? I will not deal with polarizing statements...*

And now here *I* was, feeling walked away from, minimized. In the months that followed, I wish I'd thought, or been told, to videotape my daughter's screaming or turn on an audiotape recorder – anything that would have defined for this good doctor and for me the reality of Laura's condition. My perceptions seemed to me, as a nurse, unattractively "emotional," very "hysterical mother." I knew from experience that I was becoming a nuisance to the physician, whom I not only admired and respected, but now *needed* in a way I'd never needed anyone before. I felt embarrassed, confused and unsure even of my own medical knowledge. It seemed to me that bad news was in the air, and the physician was the only one who had the power to order the tests that I could not.

It didn't help at all that at this time our families could not acknowledge Laura's difficulties. They kept saying, "She's fine, there's nothing wrong with her!" The question I wish someone had asked me is, "What is it, Kathy? What concerns you? Tell me so we can understand."

I called Laura's pediatrician and/or brought her in

> *It is not us and them. I don't want it to be us and them, I want it to be us...*
>
> *Kathy*

weekly. "She's still not rolling over," I'd report, or, "I don't think Laura *hears* – do you suppose she's screamed so much she's damaged her hearing?" As the weeks dragged by and developmental milestones were not reached, I sensed a growing sadness in Laura's pediatrician. He asked my husband and me to begin keeping a "crying log" so we could collect some data. I don't know why I didn't think of that three months earlier! With a great sense of purpose, we wrote everything down; finally we had something to do. At the end of the ten days we presented it to him with a flourish. This physician then made music to my ears when he said, "Kathy, she's crying 16 hours a day. That's just not normal." Relief – fear – jubilation – annoyance were all there for me in that moment.

Finally, I was heard.

Finally, I was believed.

And so the process of diagnosing Laura's myriad of difficulties began. The battery of developmental and medical tests concluded, when Laura was 18 months old, that she had cerebral atrophy: "Etiology unknown – prognosis unclear." At last, it seemed we knew what we were dealing with. Or did we? In the months and years since, we have come to know how much and how little the terms actually tell us. As

Laura's problems manifest themselves, new diagnoses emerge: a flavor of atypical pervasive developmental disorder, sensory integrative dysfunction, oppositional behavior disorder. I have admittedly become vigilant about my daughter's medical course. I watch her very closely. I read everything I can get my hands on regarding neurological impairment, advocacy, diet, vitamins. There is an intensity about me and the questions I pose to our physicians that might seem intimidating or threatening. This involvement and intensity I *hope* can be seen as a reflection of my commitment to my daughter, to providing her with what we all want for our children: just the very best we can give them.

I have two children: an eight and a half-year-old girl who was born at 25 weeks gestation, weighing two pounds, and a three-year-old boy, also born prematurely weighing two and a quarter pounds.

When you have a preemie, you receive certain diagnoses even *before* the birth; and in Elyse's case the predictions were bleak. Those predictions coupled with our fear was overwhelming (I've tried to remember what we were afraid of way back then, before we became seasoned veterans – hospital, doctors, nurses, smells, death). We didn't take in much of what was said to us. It was *too* overwhelming to comprehend.

Fortunately for all of us it didn't really matter. Elyse breathed on her own from the beginning and had few complications beyond a patent ductus, which closed on its own when she was about seven weeks old.

Five years later we weren't so lucky. Again we knew some of the diagnoses even before Robby was born. But we were *not* prepared for what was to come. Robby had multiple diagnoses that seemed almost incomprehensible to us.

Each new diagnosis – in the beginning – was declared "common" for a preemie, and we were encouraged to look on the positive side and reminded that time was what Robby needed; but he did not make the progress everyone expected. He had surgery for an incarcerated hernia; his head size still caused major concern; he went on steroids; he went on nasal prongs; he went back on the respirator. It became clear to everyone that there was more to Robby than we could account for. As he grew *very* slowly and got *slightly* better, we as a family began to feel more and more isolated from those around us and more and more confused. Doubt crept in. I began to feel that people – friends and professionals alike – avoided us, and certainly they avoided talking about Robby. I felt bewildered because, while no one seemed sure why Robby wasn't getting better, most everyone still assumed he would.

Finally when he was four months old, Robby came home. Our home had been set up with oxygen and we had a whole arsenal of medications to give him. He wasn't in great shape, but he was home.

Isolated at home, I lived each waking moment in fear of germs. I tried to feed Robby as much as possible, but he was a poor eater. The visiting nurse would come weekly and silently weigh him, looking grim as his weight changed one gram a week, week after week. She would quiz me on the minutiae of his care and I would feel defensive and guilty at the same time.

Then the inevitable happened. After six weeks at home, Robby got a cold. He went into immediate and almost total respiratory failure within hours of his first sneeze and was hospitalized in the neonatal intensive care unit (NICU) for two weeks, most of that time back on a respirator. The fear and despair I felt that time were obvious. But the response I received was, in many instances, less than supportive. What followed over the next two months was a seesaw of re-hospitalizations for bronchiolitis, reactive airway disease, and finally pneumonia, staph infection, and thrombo-cytopenia. We began to feel more and more anger, fear, and bewilderment. There was a growing detachment between us and the now numerous professionals involved in Robby's care. No one even named his various problems anymore. I didn't know what they were until I saw them in writing in his records much later.

When repeated attempts to extubate Robby were unsuccessful, he was transferred to a large out-of-state hospital, where he was evaluated and pronounced a candidate for cricoid surgery. I felt hopeless, and I perceived that those professionals around me did too, though no one ever said so. Things seemed *terrible*. My eyes and ears told me things were terrible, but no one was talking to me about it. No one said, "This is really bad." I felt I was the only one saying it, and that I was a weak person for having done so. I began to feel

> *For those professionals who can't be emotionally there, they can at least just listen. I don't think we expect that there will be an emotional rapport or connection with every professional, but you still expect to be heard...*

The professional can at least hear. It doesn't require superhuman power, it just requires attention.

Ruth

crazy. Here we were, with a dazzling list of treatable diagnoses, but a definite "failure to thrive" baby.

The cricoid surgery was successful, and the surgeon additionally inserted a gastrostomy tube. By now Robby had developed some new problems, most likely associated with the lengthy medical complications and procedures. He could no longer make any sounds, his G-tube was an open sore that would not heal, and he developed abnormal eye movement. More professionals entered the picture now, looking at more "pieces" of Robby. What was hard for us was that Robby had by now become a medical anomaly, a curiosity, a featured puzzle whose broken pieces were each examined by a different specialist. We as a family had to try to negotiate with each specialist, make sense of what he or she was saying, and somehow make it fit the whole picture. Often the professionals didn't agree. We felt remote from it all. I don't know if all the people involved in Robby's care ever got together to see him as a whole, but I always believed they didn't. My frustration mounted.

Almost a year old now, our "poor medical diagnosis" was discharged once again from the hospital. To me and my family, a little boy who had suffered greatly and who deserved a chance at life went home. To us he was not merely this long, complicated list of problems. We loved this baby, problems and all. We didn't know what the future would hold, but we were determined to go forward. We met resistance and disapproval in many places. Very few family, friends or professionals were prepared to meet our emotional needs. Very few people were prepared to listen to our feelings. We continued to feel isolated and alone. No one would get close enough to really hear how we felt.

Blocked communication with professionals happens when it only goes to their heads, not their hearts...

Asher was born at full term, nine pounds, a beautiful baby boy. There was nothing suspicious on the Apgar Scale. Mother and child were healthy. Still, there were concerns. Asher cried almost constantly and could not be comforted. He never molded to my body; instead, he would stiffen when held, and he *never* explored his world by placing objects in his mouth. He began walking at 13 months of age, but *never* used verbal or body language to indicate his wants. At 18 months we took him to a hearing specialist. No problems were observed and we were told to relax, that he would talk when he was ready.

Around two years old Asher began to talk, with perfect pitch and diction. He knew the alphabet, could count to ten and memorized books from beginning to end. Still, he never used any language to communicate with us. He avoided eye contact, had tantrums frequently, had odd mannerisms, and became obsessive about the window shades and electrical outlets in our apartment.

My husband and I, realizing that there are wide variations in developmental patterns, nevertheless set a limit of three years of age for Asher to "get it together." When Asher reached three years old and continued in his odd pattern of development, I took him to a public school psychologist for an evaluation.

The interaction was very difficult both for Asher and me. Asher was very anxious in this

> *The message is to open the heart. How do we open their hearts if we only speak to their heads? It doesn't get anywhere. How do we crack this egg gently?*
>
> *Marti*

unfamiliar environment. He clung to me and was not responsive to requests that he perform certain tasks. The psychologist pointed out that Asher would not make eye contact with *me*, and was not responding to *my* requests. Then he asked me how I disciplined him. I explained how I talked to him and used time-outs, and I mentioned that when he ran in front of a car, I spanked him on the bottom. The psychologist slammed his hand on the table and yelled, "You should *never* hit a child!" He recommended that I take him to the therapeutic nursery at a medical hospital in the area for a further evaluation.

I left that meeting totally traumatized. I had arrived there with great concern about my son's development. The professional's line of questioning was pointed. I felt that he had already decided that Asher was emotionally disturbed as a result of my poor parenting skills. I cried for days. I withdrew from contact with Asher as much as possible. I felt crazy. How could this be? I was thrilled to have this beautiful child, my first, at 31 years old. What could I have done, without knowing, to damage him in this way? I remained in this state of depression for three months, doing nothing to address Asher's difficulties. Finally, out of sheer desperation, I made an appointment at the therapeutic nursery.

> *Not only are we being heard, but are we hearing what professionals are saying to us? The mutuality of communication is important too.*
>
> *Pat*

Asher was seen twice before my husband and I got the diagnosis. It took every ounce of courage I could muster to go that day. The therapist delivered the original diagnosis of "pervasive developmental disorder with autistic tendencies." The first words out of his mouth are forever etched in my psyche: "I want you to know that *nothing* you could possibly have done could cause your son to do the things he does." I will always be grateful to him for these words. Here we were, hearing one of the most difficult diagnoses, and both my husband and I remember our most prominent emotion on that day was *relief*. We were *not* crazy. We had not irreparably damaged our son. There was a professional who understood his behavior and was willing to support our family through the harrowing days ahead. Our thanks go out to him.

Feeling Understood...

For families of young children with special needs, being heard is the first step toward feeling understood. Feeling understood by those same important people – spouses, family, friends, professionals – has great positive impact on the lives of these mothers and their families. They often feel isolated in facing their daily challenges. Their struggle can be made easier when their feelings are both heard and understood by those who take the time to lower their own emotional or professional barriers enough to show compassion.

The following stories illustrate the importance of feeling understood and the effect it can have on these families.

My son Jeremy is nine years old now. He was born prematurely, diagnosed with cancer at six months, had a below-the-knee amputation at eight months, was I.V. fed at home with total parenteral nutrition (TPN) for fifteen months, had chronic ear infections with tubes placed three times, has an undiagnosed connective tissue syndrome that has affected all parts of his body, from his skin and appearance to joint hyperflexibility, and has speech and cognitive delays. He has had surgery nine times, more if you include the additional procedures done to him when he was already anesthetized.

My son was not a cute baby. He had a large cephalhematoma at birth which made his head look lopsided. His developmental delays were evident early on. When he was hospitalized he was not a favorite of the nurses. The chemotherapy made him very ill, and all things considered, especially the type of cancer he had (alveolar rhabdomyosarcoma), he was very likely to die. It has been my experience that this fact makes it hard for some professionals to exhibit that caring nature that put them in the health care field in the first place. I could understand that, but it did not make our situation easier.

I was at the hospital a lot with him. I've told some people that I willed life into that baby. Medical science was giving him the best there was to offer, and my part was to have a positive, loving attitude, to utilize the unspoken mother/child bond that exists with an infant.

One evening after eight, our pediatrician stopped in to say hello after doing rounds visiting his patients. We had been admitted by the pediatric oncologist, so we were not officially considered our pediatrician's patients. He looked tired to me. Unexpectedly, he came over and asked me if he could hold Jeremy and sit and rock him for a few minutes – and he did.

At a time when other health professionals seemed to be shying away from us, this one very special, caring, humanistic act by this pediatrician has meant more to me than I could ever express in words. It came at a time when I needed to be assured by someone else that Jeremy's life was precious and valued in spite of his obvious imperfections. I felt our pediatrician was acknowledging this. We didn't talk much at the time. I also felt it was something he was doing for himself, though I do not know why. It was the most striking act of kind-

> *Maybe if professionals hear from us that we don't expect them to "fix it" they can be more comfortable with just supporting us.*
>
> *Martie*

ness by a physician I have ever seen. And, yes, he is still my son's pediatrician and will be for as long as possible.

Yesterday I had to take Robby for his pre-op appointment. He has his eye surgery a week from Friday. We had a nine o'clock appointment, and when we went in, the waiting room was full; but what really was hard for me was that it was full of sick kids. I took a well child into this germ-laden waiting room, and we waited for 45 minutes before we went into the back. And I thought, "If he gets sick now because we had to come for this pre-op appointment, I'm going to be really mad." You couldn't contain him. I tried to get him to sit on my lap and not touch anything or go near any kids, some of whom were coughing. He's almost three and he wasn't going to sit on my lap. Some kids had a toy that made noise and he wanted that toy and I was thinking, germs–germs–germs! It's hard. I wish I had spoken up, but I was dealing with other issues.

Maybe it is necessary for a professional to have a different relationship with a parent of a child with special needs, as opposed to the child who comes in with a cold. There are more global issues concerning the family with a child with special needs, and once the professional knows this, it determines the relationship. I am more demanding as a parent; I expect more from my relationship with a professional.

Over the years I've wanted to say, "Talk to *me*," to male professionals who address my husband instead of me. "I'm the one who is going to do the work. I'm the one who knows about the situation. My husband is pretending, so that he can have a relationship with you. He talks like an expert, like he's the one who deals with it everyday." I think it's because it's a man talking to a man and they were doing this male tribal bonding thing.

It's always been too important to risk the relationship with the professional by saying this. I've been afraid to jeopardize the relationship because I've needed these professionals, but I've wanted to say, "I'm the one you need to address. I'm the one who really deals with it everyday. I'm the expert. My husband may sound like the expert, but everything he knows about this he learned from me."

After Jess' Parent Evaluation Team (PET) meeting at school this year, my husband said as we got into our car, "You know, I've got to stop thinking that Jess is going to wake up talking some day." (Our daughter is nonverbal.) I dealt with that realization years ago, even though at times I wondered if I was crazy because it seemed like my beliefs about her disability were minimized by my husband and some professionals. It was a pretty lonely feeling, until over time he came to see that there really were developmental problems with out daughter.

My husband also is just becoming aware of the amount of time and emotional energy that advocacy requires. The other day after another PET, he said, "This is a full-time job. I'm amazed at how hard this job is." (Yet how many of us parents do this special-needs "full-time job" as well as doing other "paying jobs"?) I was happy to hear his acknowledgement about the demands of advocacy, yet at the same time I wanted to scream, "Where the heck have you been for the past few years? I can't believe you are just saying that now." But I kept quiet, and just thought to myself, "Learn acceptance of the difference between his level of understanding and mine. Just learn acceptance...At least he is beginning to understand..."

It's time for Jeremy's triennial PET meeting at school. Every three years there's a major assessment/evaluation PET meeting and this is the BIG ONE: the observations beforehand, and all these psych exams. It has caused me some anxiety. I know that they sense that, because the learning strategist commented on it at the meeting.

They did no psych evaluation three years ago and it really disturbed me. I was really upset about it, because they made me do something called the Vineland. It's where parents answer a lot of questions. I didn't like the questions because they asked things like, "Does he cross the street on his own?" "Does he hold your hand when he crosses the street?" Jeremy is in a wheelchair, and it really disturbed me to have to say no to these things and have this be part of his overall score...they weren't even taking into consideration physical condition. They were looking at it primarily in a cognitive way instead of including the physical as well.

So I really put my foot down and said, "This has to be done with an overview of what is out there for children with special needs to do. He isn't a typical little kid; he doesn't have little playmates, he watches the TV, that's his best friend–and that's not unusual because I know other parents whose children are in this age group and that is a lot of what they do – so how can you gauge him socially and cognitively on experiences he hasn't had simply because of the way he is?"

Well, they don't know of any test that's better. They'll do the best they can and take bits and pieces from different tests. But they *do* know that I'm concerned and I found that they were concerned about that. They heard me and understood my concerns. He's doing so well, but I said the standardized tests don't ask about what he *is* doing...and he does different things because his *life* is very different.

> *If people could just take a minute to stop and think, and understand who this individual is. If people could just stop and think.*
>
> *Lynn*

When Joel was very young, probably about a year, I needed to take my son Alex to a pediatric dentist, whom we had never seen before, because of an injury. This man's name had come up a few times in discussion with other moms because he still refers to children with Down's syndrome as Mongoloids. I felt prepared as I went in there with Joel, who had to be with us, to very calmly and eloquently inform him how damaging that term was and that we have all progressed through the years and we should try to validate the child first etc., etc. Well, sure enough, after examining Alex he turned to Joel and asked how his teeth were developing because, he said, "You know these Mongoloids often have dental problems." I was so affected by the reality of an educated professional calling my child a Mongoloid that I just sat there and said, "I know." I was not able to respond. At that point in my life, I did not have the strength to rebut, and writing this now, I realize how damaging this was for me and how I am still affected by his attitude. Perhaps now I would be better able to cope and say what I would like to say. Perhaps not. It all depends on how vulnerable I'm feeling on a particular day.

People who don't understand don't realize that they don't understand.
Ruth

I had an experience the other day at the dentist. I went in to have an old filling replaced, and just as they put all the stuff in my mouth, the dentist started asking me questions, and I couldn't respond for half an hour. With my tongue immobilized, I was really put in touch with how my daughter must feel.

She is nonverbal because her tongue doesn't work – I mean it's very uncoordinated. It really put me in touch with many different feelings. I came out of the dentist's office frustrated by the experience, but filled with compassion for my daughter. That was great. It was worth it. My tooth still aches, but it was great.

I don't know if professionals realize how much their interactions with us impact our families. Because we are in some ways, not really more fragile, but more vulnerable in certain ways because of our children's problems, professionals impact us greatly. They need to know how great that impact is and how interdependent we are. They need our information and we need their information. We need to share as mutual partners.

I saw an old friend who has become a public health nurse and is someone whose child had cancer when Jeremy had cancer. We had started a parent's group together. Anytime you see a parent who had a child with cancer when you did, you hug them and just pick up where you left off. We hadn't seen each other probably for five years, and there she was telling me about how her son had residual effects from his sister dying and went to the hospital psychiatric unit. I'm telling you, the gut stuff that comes out in two minutes because of what you've been through...I mean, that relationship automatically comes back. It's like you are war veterans. It was just amazing.

A friend of mine, who is my daughter's Girl Scout leader, was talking to me once about Jessica. And she wanted to find, but she didn't know, the right words. She was afraid that she would say the wrong words when talking to me about Jessica and her disability. I think people's fear of saying the politically incorrect thing stops communication.

I said to her, because I knew her heart was in the right place, "The words don't bother me as much as the intention behind the words, so use whatever words come to your mind so that we can talk." There is something there about getting hung up on the words, even if the understanding is present.

It was not until my daughter was five years old and undergoing a developmental team evaluation that a doctor said to me, "This must be difficult for you. How are you doing with all of this?"

I remember feeling so surprised by this question that it brought me to tears. They were not tears of anger, but of relief that someone was looking beyond all of the deficits in my daughter's development and venturing into the realm of exploring her disability's impact on the rest of the family.

I know that this kind physician cannot "fix" my feelings of grief, but somehow just asking the question brought me some healing that day. It's as if my grief is a sore that I keep to myself and rarely expose. However, this physician's question gave the sore an opportunity to be open to the air and heal. On that day, I did not need to "stuff" my grief away and hide it from the doctor. My thanks go out to that doctor. He understood that a child's disability really becomes the whole family's challenge. Thank you for asking.

I remember an interesting experience. A nurse in the neonatal intensive care unit (NICU), who I talked with recently, recalled a time when I abruptly left the unit. She had told me that Robby had a fever, and I just couldn't take any more. I knew that meant

> *Even if what we are saying isn't true, it's still real; it's my perception, it's truth for me.*
>
> *Lynn*

that something else was going wrong, and her perspective on it was so different from my perspective. I mean she thought, "He just has a fever, why are you running out of here?" But to me it wasn't just a fever, it was the straw that broke the camel's back; and her perspective was so different...

My first real acknowledgement that something was different came when one of our doctors arrived to examine our son, Joel. Those next hours of my life will always be etched in my mind. Those moments of first hearing the news will be replayed again and again; I just can't stress enough how important a time this is. Fortunately, our physician was very sensitive and compassionate, and did a wonderful job of making this awful moment in our lives a time of hope.

It was Easter morning, and unfortunately my husband had returned home to gather our other two children and to share the good news of the birth of his new son with our closest friends. So I was alone when our pediatrician came in for the initial exam. At first I thought nothing of his questions about Joel's appearance being different from that of our other two children, and even joked about the fact that we had finally gotten a child with a small nose. When he finally shared his suspicions with me that Joel had Down syndrome, he was holding the baby.

The warm memories of his caring and concern helped carry me through many of the difficult times ahead. This was a friend, not just a professional doing his job. We will all be eternally grateful for what he gave to our family in those next few hours, days, and months. He hugged us, cried with us, and gave us his time, all of which we needed so desperately.

I was immediately moved into a private room, and for me that was very important. I had only needed to listen to my roommate make one phone call to be convinced that I simply could not bear to listen to another person share their joy right now. My world

> *Some people say that the order of words is not important, but to me it's very important. Joel is not a "Down syndrome child." He's a child, first and foremost. He just happens to have Down syndrome.*
>
> *Lynn*

had just fallen apart. I had been on top of the world with my wonderful Easter gift one moment, and suddenly crashed to the depths the next. My husband finally arrived at the hospital and our doctor was there to tell him the news and to hug him, cry with him, and answer his questions. I remember being vividly aware of the fact that we were keeping the doctor from his family on this special day, but was so very thankful for the time he was willing to give us.

The days I spent in the hospital were a time when rules were bent a bit and the staff was sensitive to what I needed. There was one afternoon when I think there were about 15 people in my room. I'm thankful that they were allowed in because I needed their support right then. Nurses made me feel pampered by insisting on my getting rest, by offering information and support, and also allowing quiet, alone time. I realize that it's often difficult to know what to say, but I appreciated those people that took the risk and didn't avoid me.

Periodically, Robby must undergo a developmental assessment. The setup for the assessment is termed an "arena evaluation": a team of five specialists in child development sit in a small room while a child performs prescribed tasks. It is impersonal and cold. It is a stressful situation; it is clinical. At the end of the assessment, each of the five specialists speaks briefly about her/his findings.

On one such occasion, the psychologist was the last to speak. She had listened to everyone else and the words they kept using to describe Robby – that he had caught up and was doing things that were appropriate for his age, but that it was now the *quality* of what he was doing that wasn't quite where they wanted it to be. When it was her turn, this psychologist said, "I just want you to know that I've listened to all of you talk about the quality of this or that, but I'll tell you what I see. I see a very well-adjusted, very social little boy. The bottom line is that that stuff is important, but it's not all of who Robby is. He isn't just how he moves, or how he speaks, or how well he can manipulate his fingers. There is a person inside too."

Her comments did a lot for me. I didn't feel like I was somehow taking home an invalid, a child who hadn't made any progress at all. She's right, they can assess all that, but Robby is Robby. He's very social and likes people. He's okay. I was really happy that she was there to balance the picture. She took the focus off all of those negative things.

Life Amplified...

Daily life for families of children with special needs is filled with challenges of an intensity far greater than for most families. This intensity is not only far greater, but is also more constant and prolonged, making life a continuous roller coaster of events with very emotional highs and extremely frustrating lows. Every aspect of these families' lives is affected; even seemingly "everyday" events of life have potential to become major crises.

The stories included here give testament to the amplified nature of having a child with special needs.

Everything seems magnified when you have a child with a disability: the pain, the frustration, the sadness...A simple, everyday situation is often so much more for us. We are confronted with our "life" in so many varied ways. Fortunately though, the same is true for the joy and the pride. When Joel spontaneously says, "I love you Mommy," I can't begin to express the effect that has on me. I remember wondering if I would ever hear him say those words. What joy it brings that he utters them so freely and with such heartfelt meaning.

> *We are all riding a constant wave of emotion, and that is difficult to maintain.*
>
> *Sue*

It's all so magnified. I've never had so many deep and dark moments as I have had with Laura. But I've also not had any more glorious moments than I've had with Laura. And they are not the opposite of each other. Most times they are all there together in an instant. One couldn't exist without the other. It is as wonderful as it is *because* of the very nature of its negativeness. If it wasn't *so* bad, then it wouldn't also be *so* glorious.

Something which I find disturbing is people who say things to me that parents of non-disabled children wouldn't tolerate. For example, "Does she go to the bathroom by herself? Do you still have to wipe her?"

Would you ask that of a mother of another eight-year-old child? There is an implied permission which says that I am even more vulnerable than I think I am. It's as if I am not going to be offended by that, but I am. I *am* offended.

I remember someone saying to me once, "Because of Laura, I think your family has to look at things a little more carefully. You might also want to look at some of the specific issues, like co-dependency." Those kind of comments make me angry. Another person, a dear friend of mine, said to me one time, "I think these are issues that you will need to bring to your therapist, you know, your enablement, your co-dependence, your rigid style..."

It makes me feel exposed, with no privacy. It makes me mad.

It's so hard, when you have a child with special needs. Every facet of your life is put under a microscope at some time. Because we have children with special needs and we need to use some professionals more, it's as if it gives them liberties to come in and examine everything. It's really, really hard to have to deal with that all of the time, over and over and over...It frustrates me.

Having a child with special needs is motherhood magnified.

Lynn

Two of my kids go back to school today and Joel goes tomorrow. The closer it gets, the more I realize how nervous I am. Sometimes I'm just in the car and it pops into my head, and I burst into tears. It's all very emotionally charged. That's it. It's very unsettling. I keep thinking he's ready, but it's very different with Joel. The difference is really striking me. I am not the kind of parent that cries when my kid goes to kindergarten. It's just that it's the accumulation of five years of effort. I really look forward to him going to kindergarten, but it's so different this time. I'm scared for him.

Laura lost a tooth yesterday, which seems like it should be a simple thing to deal with. I mean, she's lost other baby teeth. There have actually been 18

teeth lost between my two children. She came home and said, "Mom," – and it was such a nice "normal" mother moment – "Mom, I lost a tooth today." And I said, "Oh, Lishy, that's just great! Show it to me." So, she reached into her bag and said, "Well, I put it in this envelope." But the envelope was all torn up and there was no tooth, and she hit the roof, she just trashed the kitchen. She had this unbelievable temper tantrum, yelling, "Stupid, jerk tooth!" She just sort of went nuts. I was at a loss about what to do, how to help her. So I decided to forget all the work I've done on healthy boundaries. I went into the bedroom where I keep the kids' old teeth, and I just sort of threw one out there on the floor.

Laura was still screaming "Stupid, jerk tooth"...and then suddenly, "My tooth!" I said, "See, it was there all the time." But, of course, I was still having an anxiety attack over the tooth. So I said to my husband when he got home, "She's lost a tooth. It's not the actual tooth, but make a big deal about it." Then I said, "You know, its really important to me that of the 18 teeth lost between *our* two children, you have never been the tooth fairy. I think it's sexist and exploitive. And I would really prefer for you to put the tooth fairy money under the pillow tonight." He just kind of nodded and mumbled. So I said, "You know, the pattern of doing things in this marriage is that I just go ahead and do these things, the same way I prepare the taxes or prepare for an individualized education program (IEP) meeting. I really think that this is a system problem. I am not going to put that money under her pillow." So he snorted an okay. Well, he went to bed and fell asleep. At two o'clock in the morning I am up agonizing over what to do about this tooth. I thought, "Damn it, I'm not going to put that money under the pillow, I always do that stuff." But guilt nagged at me: "It's Laura who will pay the price if I don't...Oh, I hate this. All the marriage therapists in the world would say that I contribute to this sick system by going ahead and enabling it." So, I told myself to sit on my hands and not put it under her pillow.

The next morning, Laura came downstairs and I said, "Hi" and she said, "The tooth fairy didn't come last night. Was I bad?" I said, "No, you weren't bad. Are you absolutely certain that the tooth fairy didn't come?" She said, "Yes, my tooth was bad." So, I said, "Gee, that's too bad, go in and go to the bathroom," and I grabbed a damn dollar and went upstairs, took the tooth and put the dollar there. I was so angry at my husband. He said to me that morning, "Want to go out for a cup of coffee?" I felt like saying, "Drop dead!" But I just said, "Yeah, I'll go out for a cup of coffee." When we got there I said, "You tell me why. Tell me why *I* always do it." And he said, "Well, it didn't occur to me." I said, "I know that. I know that. Tell me something new. Tell me something I don't know, like it was a low priority. Tell me *something*. I felt heartbroken for her this morning. And I can't say to her, well, it was Daddy's turn to be the tooth fairy. I feel it's tremendously unfair."

In the marriage counseling that we have had, they say, "Just don't do it. Just sit on your hands, button your lip." So, I did, until the very end. It didn't occur to Laura when we first went back upstairs. She said, "Oh, she came!"

I had had a knot in my stomach about the tooth from the minute she came in the door. I had thought it was a nice mother-daughter moment, you know – capture this, this is a "Hallmark" moment. But it went bad so quickly. My son, who was in the kitchen with us, put on a leather jacket (which I have said he can only wear to play in), a baseball cap backwards, and stuck a clip-on earring on his ear, and said, "I'm getting out of here...this house is crazy." It's

It is important not to forget the child underneath all of the diagnoses.

Sue

like he was seventeen, even though he's really only nine. He was doing this while she was trashing the kitchen, and I just stood there and thought "Hallmark." It was awful.

Whenever anything bad happens in my life, my response is to examine the circumstances and try to determine what, if anything, I have contributed to the situation. When my son, Asher, was diagnosed with autism/pervasive developmental delay (PDD), I anguished over my possible role in this disability: Was it something I ate when I was pregnant? Was it that severe allergy I suffered in my seventh month? Is it genetic, did he inherit it from me? Was it the protracted labor and C-section delivery? Or was I merely a woefully inadequate mother?

As time went by, and I became educated about autism, the urgency of those questions faded. The challenges of raising a child with autism required much of my time and energy. My focus became survival – survival by whatever personal re-

Why does the school need me so much? I think about this a lot. Do they think I know what I'm doing? I don't, but I don't want to tell them that.

Kathy

sources I could bring to bear in this all-out war against autism, the enigma that denies me a full and satisfying relationship with my first-born son.

Often my personal resources (patience, in particular) have been taxed to the point of complete exhaustion. Often I did not recognize the person I was becoming. I had no idea I was capable of this kind of anger, even rage. A parent in my support group shared a fleeting thought – a wish that her "impossible" child would die. I understand the pressures that push a parent to this point, this desperation. Although I *never* wished that Asher would die, I frequently wished that for myself. A wish to end the sadness, the anger, the total frustration and constant tension.

Children with autism, thankfully, sometimes experience a latency period. For several years, our family was able to settle into a reasonably predictable routine, able to enjoy the things most families take for granted but which had previously been impossible for us. Asher's meltdowns had previously been unpredictable and, as often as not, tied to activities that the rest of the family found enjoyable: playgrounds, car rides, trips to the mall, waking up from a nap, and driving down "the wrong" road to our destination, were all impetus for hours of screaming.

Just when I began to think I might be able to reclaim my life and a modicum of sanity, Asher's "latency period" ended with a bang. Adolescence reared its ugly head in the form of severe anxiety and suicidal depression. Once again, as the crisis loomed, I examined my role in this bad time.

> *The issue of control is a big one, because you can't control any of this process. Fathers feel like they ought to be able to take care of their families and make everything all right, and when they can't, it's very devastating.*
>
> *Martie*

Asher's depression seemed to be centered around his need (now apparent for the first time) to break through his isolation, to have friends. I had requested a "circle of friends" program at school for Asher the previous year, but was unsuccessful in getting it included in his Individualized Education Program (IEP). Should I have pushed the school harder? Would it have made a difference? What else could I have done?

In this case, I believe my self-examination was productive. Not through self-blame and guilt, but through putting together future plans and assuring that Asher's need for peer association would be addressed, both in school and at home. However, this process of self-examination related to raising a "challenging" child can too often become all-consuming and nonproductive. Any day, everyday situations can evoke this thought process and it looms over us. Life becomes too much. It's too much.

It affects the relationship I have with my neighbors. It's easier for them not to get to know me or like me because we are so different, because of Jeremy. He is visibly very different. It pours over into everything. The hard part as a parent is that we are the ones, every time, who just have to keep picking ourselves up and putting on that strong face and going ahead. It matters, though; it hurts. Sometimes you think you'll get used to it, but you don't ever get used to it, and it just keeps happening, over and over, and it's hard.

What do you do when you live in a world with other people, and other people don't know and don't understand? A lot of the time I think it's because of the way they have been raised in this culture. Rather than just thinking, "Well, I'm going to go over and get to know this kid and family," they are really uncomfortable. They don't know what to say. They don't know what to do. It puts a lot of responsibility on us as the parents. My whole personality has changed as a result of this. I told my older son, "I know you get picked on because of your brother, but there are still a lot of good people out there. You just go out and find the good people and forget about the rest." I try to model that myself, and it helps. Find the good ones and focus on that.

> *Why segregate kids with special needs, or even congregate them? Why not integrate them into regular settings, like the school classroom, and be inclusive? It seems almost immoral not to include children with special needs in the community.*
>
> *Martie*

We had a situation once where someone came to our house and he had this beautiful Stetson cowboy hat. It was a wonderful hat. He could see Laura eyeing the hat so he said, "Oh, well, my daughter wants this hat too, but I have very special rules about my hat." He was very understanding.

Laura, however, didn't give a hoot about his rules. She just didn't, she couldn't. She had jelly on her hands and she went for the hat. He got to it first and he gave her this beautiful long explanation about why she couldn't have the hat, thinking that it would mean something to her. But it meant nothing to her. He had talked to her, related his feelings, and done it all right. But, she did get the hat and he took it right back from her. She didn't understand, she wasn't able to care about his way of thinking. That's the imperative. That's the amplification.

Having the flu is certainly "mainstream" enough. No matter who you are, you get sick once in a while. It sounds commonplace, to be expected, something that happens to everyone and is just no big deal. Right? Wrong!

Flash to the bathroom one cold rainy evening. My six-year-old daughter, Laura (who has cerebral palsy and developmental delay), followed on my heels as I struggled to suppress the retching that my stomach flu was causing. Laura was screaming at me, alarmed: "Are you gonna be sick? Are you gonna throw up?" I knew I was in trouble, but was thinking, "Can I get her out of here before I vomit?", knowing all too well of Laura's sensory integration dysfunction, which makes auditory and visual stimulus just overwhelming for her.

The inevitable happened. I was sick into the toilet, and Laura began to feel scared and struck out, wildly thrashing and out of control. She took off her glasses and began hitting me on the head with them, over and over again. I was trapped over the toilet, incapable of stopping my nausea, trying to cover my head and deflect her strikes, while all the time trying to protect her from losing her balance and falling on top of me. Even as I was vomiting and actually causing her agitation, I had to keep trying to support her to keep her from falling. I had to stay over the toilet and yet near her; and the blows to my head never let up.

I couldn't figure out where the hell my husband was. Our whole house is tiny, just six rooms; he *had* to hear this going on! I tried to yell, "Marc!" but was so sick that I only got out the "Ma..." before another bout of nausea came over me. Laura was totally out of control. The glasses by now had cut my head, and a small trickle of blood dripped over my eye and into the toilet. I remember hearing myself think, "My God,

These are everyday experiences, but they are not everyday experiences for families with special needs. They are everyday experiences with a twist.

Sue

she's going to kill me," and absolutely hating my husband for not helping me.

When the vomiting finally stopped, I was able to grab Laura's arms and restrain them, taking the glasses out of her tiny, white-knuckled fists. I was able to call Marc, who relieved me of her so I could try to pull myself together.

I left that little bathroom that rainy evening a different woman. Before that incident, I'd thought...no, I'd *known*, that I could handle, and handle well, whatever challenges Laura presented to me. That night, I knew *nothing* any more.

I often wonder if we parents hesitate to talk about the really bizarre stuff because we assume we're alone. My guess is that we're not.

Sometimes when bad situations arise, they are the result of a combination of uncontrollable circumstances and simultaneous stress-related reactions. Take my long-awaited trip to Arizona. For several months prior to my departure, Asher had been in a crippling depression. Our attempts to relieve his symptoms with a series of medications had resulted in severe behavioral problems.

It was not uncommon for his teacher or social worker to call me at work two or three times a day seeking direction. Even worse, his obsessive/compulsive nature had risen to new heights, now verging on the unlawful. He would stay up till 2:00 a.m. making threatening phone calls, lighting fires, and opening anybody's car door to check the serial number.

The tension in our household was unbearable. Clearly, I was in need of a break and the trip to Arizona was a potential godsend. If I had written a diary of my experiences around this period of time, it might have read something like this:

April 22:
Only 48 hours before I leave for Arizona – I can hardly wait! I hope Asher doesn't burn the house down while I'm gone.

April 23:
I dropped the car off for an oil change after work today. Fifteen minutes after I got home, Asher fell against the counter while spinning the cat and got a deep gash under his eye. My car was in the shop and Brian (my husband) was unreachable by phone. He finally got home and we took Asher to the emergency room. Four stitches and a tetanus shot later, we came home.

April 24:
Time to go to the airport – my car was still in the garage and Brian was late coming to pick me up. Finally, he arrived. I brought out my carefully packed suitcase and set it down. The rear door of Brian's station wagon was locked. I went in to get the rest of my luggage and placed it in the back seat.

Hurry! We all piled into the car and Brian backed up – right over my suitcase! I had no other suitcase, so Zach (my youngest son) ran next door to borrow one from our neighbor. Brian took this time to drive to a nearby gas station for a fill-up, and discovered that his car had no brakes!

I ran home and called our mechanic to get my car off the lift while Brian, very carefully, "eased" his car back to our garage. I then lunged into the back seat of the car to stuff my meticulously ironed clothes into my neighbor's much smaller suitcase.

At the mechanic's we switched cars and drove at break-neck speed toward the airport. As we were driving along Brian checked the time and commented that I might not make the flight. My ticket read "non-refundable." That was it! I dissolved into tears. Zach, seeing me upset, also began crying. Brian started swearing.

Unbelievably, we made it to the airport in time for me to catch the flight.

April 25:
Arizona is wonderful, the conference is terrific, the hotel is fabulous! I'm sick. My nasal passages are clogged, my ears are blocked up, my stomach is upset, and I have diarrhea. I hope Brian is watching Asher – day *and* night.

April 28:
I arrived back home today. Thank God, I still have a house and family to come home to.

May 5:
Asher was expelled from school today. He was like a caged animal when I arrived to pick him up. Please God, let me have my son back.

This diary reveals my trip to Arizona as something like a Three Stooges movie, in many respects, utterly ridiculous and unbelievable. The interplay of uncontrollable, successive events and stress-related reactions catapulted me into the world of "slapstick tragedy." I was a stress-driven individual, temporarily sucked into a black hole.

> *I just don't know what "normal family" is. I'm not there yet. I always wonder, am I like every other family?*
>
> *Kathy*

At this point in my life, I can look at that whole situation and be a little kinder to myself. After all, who could live this life and do it better?

On the last day of school this year I had a meeting with a consulting occupational therapist (OT), Laura's regular OT, and the case coordinator at school. We were sitting in this room, four women, when the consulting OT, holding my hand, started saying things like, "You know, Kathy, you really need to develop some interests outside of school, we've had you here too much. This is too much for you. And I'm just concerned. You deserve a life." I said, "You know, I'm really uncomfortable with the assumptions and projections you are making about me. I *have* a life. I have a very rich, rewarding life that you know nothing about. I can't believe you are talking to me like this." But she continued, "After this meeting, we'll go out in the hall, and we'll talk about your relationship with your husband." She actually said that.

I couldn't believe it. I couldn't believe that she could be so demeaning to me...so unprofessional and unethical. It's got to be illegal or something that she did that. I just got up and left. But even as I left, something gnawed at me, something bothered me right to my very core. If something gets me, really gets me, I need to look at it and say, "Why is this getting me? Yes, she did violate me all over the place, but can it be that maybe there is a kernel of truth in what she said that is really making me mad?" I think it's true that parents of children with special needs probably struggle to some degree in their intimate relationships. It was no veiled inference that, "We'll talk about your relationship with your husband." It implies all of this sexual stuff, and I thought, "This is bugging me because she's really getting me where it hurts. My womanhood, my wifehood." I even felt that my sexuality was tapped a bit. Was she inferring that I don't "service" my husband enough or something? I was just so mad, so wounded, and yet there was something there that got my wheels turning.

I guess there are really two issues here. One is the inappropriateness and abusive nature of what she said. The other is what it meant to me. That woman took advantage of what she might have known about a woman like me. She used what she knew to hurt me. She used it...she used it.

Asher wears a baseball cap to cover up the patches of hair he has pulled out of his head. He began pulling hair out during the time he was taking anafranil, a medication prescribed for obsessive/compulsive disorders. There is a rule at school that students cannot wear hats. They intend to enforce it in Asher's case. I cannot believe I have to fight this battle.

It is always music to my ears when I hear a health professional or a teacher acknowledge the different aspects of my daughter that are positive. It acknowledges her wholeness, rather than her brokenness.

So often I hear about all of her deficits: her language abilities are this far behind, her motor skills are that far behind. I know that she will always be behind in many areas. But it also brings balance to the picture when someone, other than myself, can see the greater picture of my daughter, beyond her disability. She is so much more than someone who can't talk. I love hearing from her doctor, "She sure does have a great sense of humor and determination," or from her teacher, "She is such an asset to our class. She is really teaching the other children that there are so many ways to communicate beyond words."

And often it may not even be the words others say, but a look that my daughter and our family receives. Eyes that offer *compassion without pity* feel so much better than the eyes that dissect our family or dissect my daughter into fragments.

> *Our children are separate individuals too, and need to be seen as more than their disability.*
>
> *Lynn*

I particularly love those anecdotal observations that are "normal kid stuff" news. When I share with the speech therapist the different things that Jessica is trying to share by signing or reenacting, and she says, "That's a normal thing for kids her age." It helps to remind me that my daughter is a "normal" kid first, who just happens to have a disability layered over her "normalcy."

My husband and I are very acutely and sometimes painfully aware of our daughter's deficits. But hearing about her strengths and our family strengths from others fortifies us, and strengthens our sense of hope.

I have a best friend who has always been supportive, and she brought her daughter over to my house. Her daughter is an adolescent, but she got Laura swinging so hard on the tire swing in the yard that she slammed her into the tree that it's tied to, and Laura was cut down the back of her head. I had gone outside twice previously to say, "Stop, it's too rough." The last time, I started running toward them, and that's when my friend's daughter pushed her into the tree.

I was really upset. I said to her, "That was too rough. I told you twice to stop and you didn't stop." I continued, "You know that Laura has disabilities that might impair her ability to stay with the swing when it's that wild. I am really upset, I'm really frightened." Well, my friend is mad at me now. She feels like I blamed her daughter, which of course I did.

In a normal situation, if it were my son that went into the tree, I wouldn't be so upset. I mean, I wouldn't have liked it if I had said to stop twice, but it's as if because I am a mother of this child with special needs, it's different. I should have been out there and it wouldn't have happened. I shouldn't have been having coffee with a friend in the kitchen. Now my friend thinks we need a time out. It's as if I'm going to lose everybody, because the situation means I can't keep my mouth shut.

After it happened and Laura was all cut up, I had her in a show that I was singing in. Originally, mothers and daughters were going to hold hands and sing for a conference on Mother's Day. Then they had the children dancing and doing cartwheels, which really upped the ante. Laura had to dress up as Dorothy and wear these little red shoes. I mean she can barely walk anyway, and now she had red patent leather tap shoes, so it was really getting crazy. So I was sitting in this rehearsal watching Laura fall, try to dance, fall again with the other kids knocking her over, when my friend came in. She said she wanted to talk to me about what I had said to her daughter. Do you know what that moment was like for me?

Here is one of the dearest people in the world to me, trying to tell me everything I did that was wrong, and there's my daughter up on the stage falling, getting knocked over, and she's already hurt from hitting the tree. I just sat there thinking, "This is crazy. This is so awful." Nobody else knew what it was like. I just sat there listening to my friend and watching my daughter fall, thinking, "Can't she see, can't she know this is awful?" It was all just so awful.

Shrieking gleefully, flying through the house without a stitch of clothing, Isaac has in a few seconds reduced Christmas to just another day.

Our tree stands center stage, truly splendid, adorned with a mass of silver and gold finery. It towers over a heap of kaleidoscope-colored packages, winking and blinking in the early morning light.

Isaac darts to and fro, a fine pink streak drawing closer and closer to the baubles, like a moth to flame. Oh, my little moth. Does he wonder why we've forested the living room? With wonder? With pleasure? The

It's like having to sit in the middle of a raging fire without a hydrant and yelling out from the pain.

Kathy

dancing lights shine in his eyes. On and off. Off and on. On again. He reaches for a light tentatively. In his hand it glows: a cool white ember.

The gifts don't get a second glance. He is not aware they contain wonderful new things, and even if he was, he would not care, precisely because they are *new*.

I wait across the room holding out his underwear. He sees me and leaps and laughs his way over to where I wait.

"Merry Christmas, Isaac," I tell him as I capture his hand in mine. "Time to go potty." He pulls on my arm. A dozen times a day I take him. A dozen times he protests. He pees in the toilet with small wails of habit.

"Try," he says looking up at me anxiously. I have said it at least a million times. He must think it's par for the course. You sit, you urinate, you say, "Try." I help him pull his underpants up over his hips. Such slim boy hips.

"Good boy, Isaac," I say as he stumbles out of the bathroom released.

I go to the kitchen to prepare something special. A Christmas breakfast. Maybe waffles with almonds and a Grand Marnier sauce, or pancakes wrapped around strawberries; or how about...and Isaac suddenly is there at the window, looking desolate. His mouth is sucking at the glass like a fish. He is searching for his bus.

"Hurry up," he calls out. "Hurry."

"No buses today, Isaac. No school." I say it softly and slowly. I tell him this every day of vacation, and still he waits for the familiar rattle of his bus, every morning like clockwork.

Bethanie and Sarah push and shove their way into the kitchen, asking, "When we can open the presents?" Bill, right behind them, still sleepy, suggests, "How about tomorrow?" and the girls groan and giggle. Isaac's eyes have not left the window.

"C'mon, kiddo," I stroke my son's shiny hair. He pulls away from the caress. I know he does not like his head touched. Sometimes for a moment I forget on purpose. "C'mon, Isaac, let's go see the nice presents."

The girls have gone ahead, making guesses at the contents. Bill is trying to prevent a massive attack on the brightly wrapped boxes. I try to coax Isaac away from the window and into the living room, without any luck. He is going on and on about trucks. Like a mantra he chants his endless litany of vehicles.

Finally I pick him up and carry him into the living room. Beth is exclaiming over a new outfit. Sarah pulls the tissue paper off a new doll. Bill sips some special holiday coffee, while Isaac decides to lie half under the tree mewing like an injured animal.

"I wish that Christmas was once a week," Sarah announces to us as she examines her doll's petticoat. "Last night I wished I'd get this doll. Did you get what you wished for?"

I made a wish. "I wish he was like other four-year-old boys, shouting over a Ninja turtle or a monster truck," I say.

"That would be too expensive," Beth says seriously. "I wish it was twice a year." Bill snorts. I open a small package.

"I wish Isaac was not autistic," Bill says. I laugh and tell him I was thinking the same thing. Wishing the same thing.

On starlit nights when I wish upon a star, and when I throw a penny in a well, that's what I wish. When I blow out the candles on my cake each year, that's what I wish.

Sarah looks up and glances at Isaac, now hidden beneath the heavy branches of the evergreen, "If everybody was autistic, people would save a lot of money at Christmas time." Yes, that was true. Isaac has yet to open a gift. Bill tries to interest him, inquiring, "What could be in the nice big box?" But Isaac wants nothing to do with the nice big box. There are one or two presents he might like. A book with his Jesse Bear. Enough the same, I think, to whet his appetite. An electronic sound effect toy. His small pile of presents remains undisturbed.

I dread it when a relative asks if Isaac likes the police car, the puzzle, the crayons, it doesn't matter what. How do I say, "No"?

Nope, nada, zip, not a one. I try to explain, but how do you explain to someone something you don't understand yourself. Isaac does not care for this Santa fest!

Yes, Virginia, we have come a ways. Isaac recognizes Santa Claus now. He once shouted Santa's name when he saw the bearded fellow. He has enjoyed having a real tree inside the house. He wails less and smiles more.

To calm himself now, he plays his answering machine messages a few dozen times; he lunges over the couch; he chortles and giggles; and he lists his vehicles for us again and again. He postures and perches like a bird, his arms reed thin, all bones, doing his own autistic ballet. He allows Bill to help him open a package hand over hand, and he discovers that bows can stick on the wall, on the TV, on us, and on and on.

Evening arrives, and with it "Star Trek." A long-awaited guest. Now something is right, expected. "Star Trek" with all of Isaac's friends: Data, Riker, Captain Picard.

"Troi," Isaac exclaims happily. This boy who never greets anyone, unless prodded, never fails to greet his television neighbors.

I am tired. The house is papered from one end to the other with little snowmen and reindeer dashing and dancing. The tree looks bereft, like a mother without her children. The girls are upstairs comparing their bounty. Bill dozes on the floor, as stuffed as the turkey was. Isaac stands inches from the screen, following every move Data makes with delight. I'm so tired. Another two hours, give or take. Another two hours till Isaac will go to bed. He is squealing now. That infantile squeal no one makes, except a baby discovering its toes, and a child with autism. I think it's joy. Joy to the world and goodwill to all men.

A blizzard has hit my kitchen. The table is covered with potatoes and a scattering of bones. Bones and a few smile-shaped pie crusts grin at me. Picard is talking. It's almost time for the Enterprise to boldly go wherever they go after seven o'clock. Another hour. Isaac is not happy. Every minute is endless. Too much excitement and noise. Isaac is yelling now. Telling us about it with his lion voice. He comes into the kitchen and grabs my arm.

"What is it? What do you want?" Am I really asking, "What do you want from me? I have given you everything I have to give. Do you want my blood? My marrow?"

Loving Isaac, living with Isaac is like living with a vampire. He sucks the life right out of you. Isaac shakes my arm, he nips the skin at my wrist.

"What?" I yell. He wants me to fix it. To make it all right. But I'm not Santa. I don't have any magic. I can't make wishes come true. Oh, but if I could. If I could, what a Happy New Year it would be.

"Night?" Isaac asks. He is a little boy again, waiting for the right answer. I tell him it is night and his smile is brighter than any Christmas tree. Time for bed. Good old bed. Same old bed. Wake up Daddy, and bid goodnight to the twinkle bright tree. Bid goodnight to Beth and Sarah. We say our lines and he says his. Tuck him in with a kiss and hug.

Downstairs to pack the turkey into the too-full refrigerator. I'm exhausted. Almost done with this day. I load the dishwasher with a million plates and forks. Bill comes in and begins to wrap leftovers. We clean up, slowly in silence, an old couple.

"Did you have a good Christmas?" Bill asks. I nod. All in all, it was a good day. Nothing unusual or out of the ordinary. I smile as he slips his arm through mine. He turns off the light. The kitchen is dark for a moment, until the light of the opened refrigerator spills across the floor.

"Are you still hungry?" I ask, amazed. Bill's face reddens as he reaches for a turkey leg.

"Naw..." He scans the contents with regret and points to the poor ravaged bird, sitting half naked on a platter. "I thought you might want to break the wishbone now?"

Why am I holding my breath? I wonder, as I shiver in the chilled air.

"No, I guess not. Tomorrow's fine. Or whenever." After all, it doesn't really matter. It's always the same wish.

Chronicity...

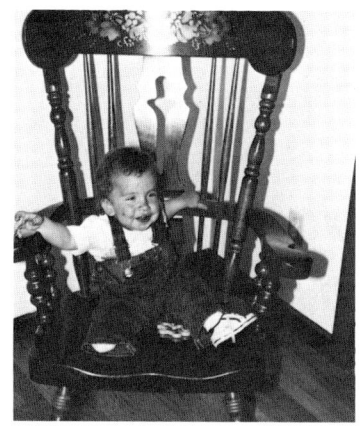

The extra challenges that result from having a child with special needs never fully go away. The nature of the situation may change, but daily life rarely if ever falls into a "normal" routine or even a predictable pattern. This constant state of heightened action or reaction, causes extra stress and tension in the family. The chronic nature of this state of being requires continuous adaptation, adjustment and compromise.

The chronicity of these challenges is evident from the experiences of mothers in the following stories.

The pain never ends for us. I can be going along just fine, appreciating Joel for who he is and receiving so much joy from him, when one little comment enters the picture and haunts me for days. I was speaking to a dad about our sons both playing T-ball the other day, when he asked his son if he knew Joel. The little boy stopped to think and said, "You mean the slow one?" At the time I laughed and said, "Yeah...that's the one!" How sad though, that "slow" will always be his primary definition. I want people to look at him and not have their first thought be "Down syndrome."

> *It's an accumulation of well-meant but inappropriate comments about our kids, comments that invalidate the pain and frustration of these more than challenging children.*
> *Kathy*

More than anything, what my husband and I would like for our son, who has autism, is what most of the world takes for granted: an opportunity to belong; to be invited to the parties of his peers; to become a welcomed part of our neighborhood, school, and community. Is it so much to ask? It seems, sometimes, that the social aloofness so typical of individuals with autism has been reinforced and solidified by the community response to such a disability. Not so long ago, these individuals were largely segregated in physically isolated residential treatment facilities. Today, many are residing with their families or in community settings. They are physically present in our towns. We have some discomfort with that, not surprisingly, since they have been hidden from our view for so long. Yes, they are present, but we have not embraced them as valued members of our neighborhoods, churches, schools, or communities. How much longer must we wait?

Joshua just started a job. We'd better say a little prayer that he'll do well. He's going to work in a shoe shop near his dad. He doesn't function well at all with a crowd of people around, he prefers to be alone. He's having it real rough. People are talking to him and he's not responding, he doesn't want to respond. He just wants to be left alone. He wants to stay in his room all day. My youngest son starts school soon...soon...not soon enough.

I think parents of children with special needs all have been through this experience It's when things are going along fine, then you need a doctor's letter or something for insurance purposes. The doctor(s) present the worst-case scenario and when you read it, you feel the same overwhelming feelings again.

> *You never really know, when a crisis happens, if this will be the one that undoes you, puts you over some undefined edge.*
> *Kathy*

Even though the letter itself is minor, just thinking about it and seeing it in writing brings it all back. It's hard; you see everything that's ever happened, which isn't what you deal with day to day. Day to day, you deal with each thing as it happens; but seeing it all together, you develop anger and despair. It reminds you of things you forgot. Then you worry those same things will come up again.

Why should we have to go through all of this? Insurance companies who have already dealt with the case should realize why, when your child reaches two years of age, you need to do certain things. Seeing it all in writing erodes your confidence and sense of accomplishment.

A while back I talked to a mother I know, and she was telling me that they put her son on Anafranil, which is the medication that Asher had been on last year, or one of them. Her son had been on it for two months at that point and was doing very well. It made him much more accessible and calmed him down. I was excited for her. For the first two weeks we had Asher on that medication, he was wonderful. Then things just deteriorated. But he really had changed a lot during those two weeks. He was chatty. He was talking to people and initiating conversations, and even though it was short-lived, it was one of the things that kept us trying other medications, hoping they could have that kind of effect on him. It was as if there was something there that we could get at.

Recently I received a letter from the same mom, who said that around Christmas time the medication became toxic for her son, that he became very aggressive and agitated, and they were having to look at putting him in a residential treatment program if they kept him on that medication. So they took him off it. He is now on no medications. It's really interesting because it's the same medication, but it took him two months to get to the same point Asher was at in two weeks. Both of us saw a real, marked improvement early on, then deterioration. It was really hard for them. But they are very relieved now, because he is off of that and all other medications, just like our son. That's where they are now, and they are relieved.

We went to New York, to my parents', in a car. For the first time ever, I really noticed Jeremy's hyperactivity. It's starting to be hard. He was so excited to go, and he didn't get to sleep before 11:00 or 11:30 every night we were there, and he was up at a quarter to five every day. Just about the time we were ready to go home, he started to settle down. Other than that, he was just off the wall. He went from one thing, to the other thing, to the other thing, never staying in one place more than two seconds. My father is not very tolerant. He doesn't know how to handle it, and it's hard to teach a sixty-year-old man new coping mechanisms. He doesn't really get it and he doesn't understand why I can't make Jeremy behave.

> *Every triumph that we have is the result of a struggle because of the special need.*
> *Martie*

We went through this with Matthew too, but medication helped Matthew, and now his behavior is wonderful. Jeremy's medication doesn't work, and that's really hard. Last spring and summer we tried different medications, and it was really frustrating because nothing helped at all; the medications actually made everything worse. They had worse side effects than the attention deficit (AD) alone, but every time the hyperactivity becomes intolerable, it makes you wonder whether to try medications again. I'm not sure this cycle is beneficial.

We're going back to my folks' at Christmas, so I tried to explain Jeremy's behavior to my mother. She gets really upset when I say this, but I said, "Our choice is to come and have you and dad accept us as we are, or not to come." She said, "Don't threaten me with that, don't say that." I said, "I'm not threatening you, that's just the way it is, that's the way we are. We are not a perfect family. We're us. You take us as we are."

Once on the way home from a weekend trip, we made a stop to look for a pizza place. There was this little shopping mall where we found one. But it was take-out only and we wanted to sit down to eat, so we walked back out to the car. We were getting ready to get into the car and go somewhere else, when we discovered Asher wasn't there. He had totally disappeared. We thought maybe he was just hiding behind a post or car or something, to surprise us. We sat in the car for a minute, waiting for him to peek out, but he didn't. We sat there for five more minutes, looking around, waiting for him to peek out. He still didn't, and I thought maybe he was into his car thing again. So, Zach and I went all through this big mall's parking lot, thinking that he was looking at cars, but he wasn't. Then we went through a department store in the mall looking for him and we still couldn't find him. We went through the electronics store and all these different stores in this mall, but he wasn't there.

A half-hour later we found him at the book store, all the way back, in the far end of the store. He really had no idea where he was. During the rest of the ride home I kept thinking Asher must have

> *There are just those things that parents think are going to unlock their child - but they don't. You sometimes think, "This is it, if we just do it enough, they'll get better." We cling to that hope.*
>
> *Kathy*

thought that I would have said no if he had asked to go the bookstore. I mean, we were all hungry and we wanted to eat, and he wanted to go to the book store, and we probably *would* have said no if he had asked. So that's the way autistic children think. It's either right or wrong, black or white, yes or no, and that's the way it is. Parents of children with autism always feel like these children were beamed down from some other planet. There is that sense. The binary reasoning is evident, like in a "Star Trek" episode.

I was talking to another mother about this, and she said her four and a half year-old son, who also has autism, disappeared once for a couple of hours. He just left the house. They were frantic. They looked all over and couldn't find him anywhere, so they called the police. The police were about ready to get the dogs to find him, because they live near all these streets, when a supermarket about a mile away from their house called about this little boy in his underwear watching the chicken rotisserie going around. All they could get out of him was "chicken" (he can't talk). They had called the police, who were already looking for him. So now this mother and her husband have put locks and alarms all over the house. They feel like prisoners, but it scared them to death. I was thinking, we had just gotten through our episode, which wasn't as bad. We *knew* Asher was somewhere at the mall. And if anybody took him, well, they'd be sorry – *they'd* soon be looking for *us*!

It's so tempting to just send Joel off to school, or camp, or whatever, and "let them deal with him." I know I can't do that. I need to be intimately involved in every part of his life. It's so different from my other two children, so much more constant.

I can say now that I survived my first parent evaluation team (PET) meeting. I am a fairly educated and assertive woman, but I was surprised that I lost sleep for the month prior to that meeting. I hope this gets easier over time. It must just be overwhelming for parents who are less educated than the "experts" or who are easily intimidated. I was also not very productive for a couple of days after the meeting. I felt wounded. I'd feed the children a frozen boxed dinner and then take a bubble bath...

One year later. Let's see, how many PET meetings have we had this year? Maybe they weren't all official PET meetings, but they all involved advocating for our daughter's educational needs. Well, I am

> *I try not to put limits on what Jessica is capable of, especially as it relates to the future. But my fears about the future are ever-present.*
>
> *Marti*

learning that trying to be Mrs. Nice Guy need not be my primary concern. My family and I are the ones who live with Jessica's disability and will for the rest of our lives. Therapists and teachers will come and go. If I let Mrs. Nice Guy interfere with my advocacy, then my daughter and the rest of us are the ones to have to live with the consequences of mediocrity.

I try to give positive strokes to the teachers and therapists working with my daughter. But I won't buy into the status quo, if it is inappropriate for my daughter's needs. I don't like confrontation. I don't like disagreements. I don't like being a squeaky wheel. However, my love for my daughter gives me the strength to do the things that are uncomfortable for me. I have survived PET meetings with our principal, our special education director, our school superintendent, and our school board. My daughter has only been in school for two years. There is a long journey ahead of us...

When Asher was thirteen years of age, he slid into an acute depression with suicidal tendencies. My husband and I took him to a psychiatrist for an evaluation, which supported our concerns about Asher's emotional state. Just prior to this, Asher had been placed on the medicine Anafranil by another physician. While on this medication, he began pulling his hair out and exhibiting agitated behaviors. The psychiatrist agreed to monitor Asher's response to the medication he was prescribing for anxiety and depression. Because our family had no health insurance at that time, we could not afford a higher level of care.

Asher's psychiatrist followed his progress for the next six months, and through three trials of different medications. Each time, as Asher reached the therapeutic level, he would become very agitated and aggressive, and exhibited compulsive behaviors and loss of impulse control. Needless to say, this made life at home and in the classroom very difficult and, at times, out of control.

> *There is no end to this. This is the way its going to be. Its going to hurt and nobody is going to like it, but you just have to keep going. It's hard.*
>
> *Kathy*

When I called the psychiatrist for suggestions on behavior management, he said he couldn't suggest any in this circumstance, and recommended that we place Asher at a local psychiatric facility until he was stabilized on the medications. Coincidentally, that same day Asher's teachers, in a meeting with me, said that they felt they could no longer deal with his behaviors. Asher's psychiatrist then chose to bail out as well. He said that Asher was the most involved child in his practice and that we could not afford to pay him to provide the level of care that Asher needed. He said that if his colleagues knew he was only following Asher's medications (this involved at least one monthly meeting and regular phone calls) when Asher needed so much more, they would think he was crazy. He did not feel comfortable with the arrangement.

> That's what keeps you going - the love - and being more aware of the little steps that are big steps.
>
> Lynn

So we were left with a school system that expelled Asher within three weeks for behaviors related to his disability (illegally, abridging his civil rights), and no doctor. The psychiatric facility was out of the question; we felt that would not be in Asher's best interest. So my husband and I decided to stop all of Asher's medication; and within two weeks he was greatly improved.

We felt frustrated, angry, and abandoned at the worst possible time.

J.B. (Joel Bowman) was born on April 19, 1977 by C-section. As his doctor held him up for me to see, he kicked his legs, flopped his arms, and howled nonstop for twenty minutes.

J.B. was always an active baby. He did not like to sleep more than two out of 24 hours. He was a projectile vomiter, and did not reach normal birth weight until three months of age.

J.B. was very busy at all times. By eight months, he could flip himself out of his crib to crawl on the floors and pull himself up to anything unreachable. By nine months, he was a walking terror! We turned his crib upside down to keep him confined and safe at night.

At age five J.B. had his first grand-mal seizure. It lasted three hours and 21 minutes. He was admitted to the intensive care unit (ICU) at the hospital. He was in a chronic, nonstop seizure state at that point.

> *It really does come back to us. It's us. Even with our husbands. What it comes down to is that we always have to be at our best and handle it somehow. We just have to handle it.*
>
> *Kathy*

Once he was stabilized, he had regressed to an infantile stage. He was non-verbal, non-walking. These abilities subsequently came back, slowly. After two days in the ICU, he was transferred to the pediatric ward.

After another two days, the staff decided that J.B. could go home, with 24-hour monitoring by me. From this point, my world began to revolve around J.B.'s condition. Medical issues were paramount through school age. After many trials of various medications, one was found that improved his condition.

Once J.B. entered school, school issues became the focus of my world. I learned early on that the only chance J.B. had of surviving in school was for me to advocate for him. Every year, every classroom has become a struggle for understanding and of advocating to meet his special needs.

It has been nearly 14 years since my son's birth, and 11 years since we first heard the diagnosis of autism. My husband and I now find that we have more time and space to consider the philosophical and political ramifications of such a disability. As most families having children with pervasive developmental disorder (PDD)/autism discover, the diagnosis is just one of the first events in a lifelong cycle of chronic crisis. Our family discovered after a time that we had become so acclimated to the unpredictability of living with a child with autism, that we had, in some way, lost all sense of the bizarre. You mean all families don't have toddlers who carry around extension cords instead of teddies, scream inexplicably for hours, and spend days raising and lowering the shades? "Autism, the early years" was a blur of doctors, frustrated behavior-management plans, and concomitant feelings of parental inadequacy. Because loud noises, large open spaces, and a variety of unpredictable occurrences all added up to long spells of inconsolable crying and screaming, we found our lives telescoped, becoming smaller and smaller. With so many noxious stimuli to avoid, our world was controlled by the desire to just "stop the screaming." However, slowly, imperceptibly, over time we did recapture a semblance of a "normal" life. Milestones were reached, public school education began. It seemed that at last our lives would slip into a

> *A child with a disability seeps into every crack of our lives. The professionals try to compartmentalize it. They don't realize that it filters into everything.*
>
> *Marti*

predictable, albeit unusual routine.

It was not to be. The next crisis loomed. Children with autism frequently do not seem to need or desire contact with other people. Our child avoided contact with other children, rarely responding in any way to their attempts to communicate. He developed language, but apparently chose not to use it to maintain human contact. As his mother, I was greatly saddened that Asher was not interested in developing friendships. What would his life be like without friends? Over the course of time, I was able to adjust to the idea that if Asher had no friends, it was his choice, and as such he was choosing an "alternative lifestyle," one that could have merit for him. (How high-minded.)

At twelve years old, a breakthrough of sorts occurred, a breakthrough that led to the next crisis. Glimmers of change began to appear. Asher complained of "feeling left out" at family gatherings. He made feeble and usually inappropriate attempts to get the attention of other children. It became increasingly clear that Asher was not content in his isolation. He needed and wanted friends, although his behavior was so bizarre and contradictory that it often confused and repulsed even the most benevolent of his classmates. A severe and debilitating depression overtook Asher that winter, worsened by the paradoxical effects of the medications prescribed to treat it.

When, at last, the depression lifted and we were able to reclaim our son, my husband and I became committed to providing for Asher what he had clearly demonstrated he needed: assistance in making friends. We had previously tried to interest Asher's teachers and special education director in the "circle of friends" concept. They saw no value in this, since it did not address academics, which they clearly viewed as their focus.

Although our attempts to address Asher's socialization skills in our school system had been previously rebuffed, we renewed our efforts. After all, Asher had chosen in the fourth grade to remove himself from his self-contained classroom. He had clearly demonstrated the intellectual ability to perform in a regular educational setting. He was expressing (however inappropriately) a desire to fit in socially with his peers and he deserved an opportunity to become a real part of his school community at last. And for the first time, my husband and I dared a vision of our child as a fully functioning member of the community.

Since Asher would be entering the junior high school in the fall, we investigated the program to determine what kinds of modifications would be desirable and how services could best be delivered. I was stunned when the guidance counselor confided in me that "not all teachers at the junior high are willing to modify their classes" to accommodate children with special needs. A stone wall. How could this be? It became evident to us that Asher could not be successful in a school program that was not committed to making modifications for his special needs.

> It's damage control. You stick your finger into the hole in the dike. Some days it's the best you can do. But sometimes I look at my life and think, "Gee, is my life just about damage control?" Right now, I think it is. That's okay, it will be different at some point.
>
> Kathy

I experienced a range of feelings about this situation: first, gratitude to the guidance counselor who was courageous enough to expose this situation, preventing a disastrous placement and saving me much time and wasted effort. I also felt both frustration at and sympathy for the teachers, who would deprive my son of his rightful place among his peers. I recognized that many of these teachers believed themselves unequipped to teach a child with autism; they were afraid of the unknown. Lack of educational and administrative support and special education consultation undoubtedly played a crucial factor in their position.

Over time, our feelings of frustration, rather than diminishing, coalesced into righteous indignation, even outrage. Although my son has much to gain from being in an inclusive setting, the other children have just as much to gain by knowing Asher. My son is a virtual learning lab for the concepts of patience, compassion, and especially problem-solving, not to mention the fact that at age thirteen he's reading at the first-year college level.

We are not heroes. We get up every morning, and we don't want to do it either. It is not heroic, believe me.

Martie

We have since decided that our lives will never slip into a predictable routine. We will always be faced with situations where we will have to advocate for our son. His autism is lifelong, with all of its predictable unpredictability. We must, therefore, always expect the unexpected, and expect progress to be slow, sometimes painfully slow. We are moving against a social tide.

Coping...

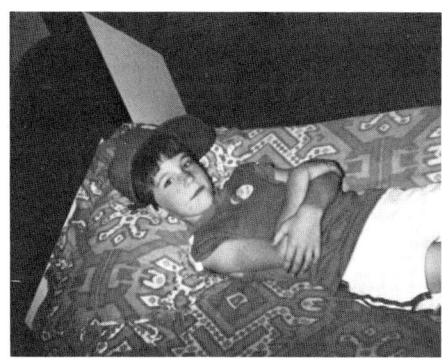

All families have multiple and varied ways of coping with life's demands, but for families of children with special needs, successful coping strategies are absolutely essential in dealing with the daily challenges they face. These families must not only cope with the demands placed on them by their child, but with the attitudes and behavior of other family members, acquaintances, school officials, and a myriad of other people, whose responses are different because of the presence of this special child. One of the most successful ways to cope is to seek and accept support from others – family members, friends, support groups, professionals and many others – but especially from those parents in similar situations.

The value to these families of supportive relationships or a network of support is evident in the mothers' stories shared here.

There are times when the pressures, the worries, the responsibilities seem overwhelming. At times like this, I know I need to seek one of my friends who is in a similar situation. As supportive as my other friends can be, there are things they just can't possibly understand. I sometimes need to talk to someone who really "knows," who's been there.

The reality is we all have bills and someone in the family has to work and have a job. And for the husband to have the job and be good at it means that I do everything on the homefront. That's what it takes, but it doesn't mean that I can't be resentful. That is the reality, but I don't have to like it.

What helps me is to talk about it, because sometimes it's not easy. My husband can stay away and keep a distance from it, which makes it easier for him, but it's harder for me. That's just the way it is, but it helps to talk about it.

I think there comes a point where we really need to collapse on someone, to let all of our stuff out...

And if we feel loved and accepted and cared for, even though we feel lousy about things, that's important, because we are always the ones who are giving.

Lynn

It's really helpful being in a support group and reflecting your feelings with other people. There are lots of other parents out there who feel the same way. There is not a better way to get that understanding. It's not as if I want people to commiserate with me all of the time; yet sharing with others keeps me going. The mutual support that I get from people in similar circumstances is empowering.

I know that there are good times and there are bad times, but the mutual support of knowing that other people are going through the same ups and downs is what really helps me. It's how we all cope.

The men-women issue; the husband-wife issue; the mother-father issue; it's not clean. It's not an issue where everyone can say it's because my husband has to go to work and work X number of hours, it's messier than that. It's very individual according to what our marriages are.

What I think about is my husband leaving a Parent Evaluation Team (PET) meeting early so that he can go play golf. There is a difference there. But my husband may need to leave that PET meeting to the same degree I need to go to a support group. This is all a question of degree. Somewhere in all of that is the way it is. There are degrees here. It's different...It's just different.

It takes a lot of energy. The time I have carved out for myself is getting filled with endless "stuff." I just need to accept the fact that I'm never going to get much time. This *is* my work right now, or the bulk of it. We average one to two meetings a week at school. I think it's important, but it's also irritating that it has to be followed this closely.

We went to an autism family retreat with Asher and it was really wonderful. It was really nice to be with a lot of the people from my support group that were there, and of course, Asher's autism consultant as well as other people. It was like old home week, with all the people that we knew. They had a respite worker that had worked with Asher, and one other

I've found that advocating for my daughter, being a case manager, has been challenging, very difficult and intimidating at times. But I've had support along the way from people who listened to my feelings and gave me input as to what worked for them. I needed and continue to need those other people. I can't do it alone.

Marti

boy with autism, so it was really manageable for him. It was just really nice to be away. There was a sibling group for Zach, and he didn't want to leave. He loved it. It was really nice for our family just to get away. It felt really good.

Just after Joel was born, the fabric of my life was dipped in a dye of "Down syndrome," and it wasn't a very pretty color. But the years have softened the shade, and although I never would have chosen it, I can now see the beauty in it and truly take pleasure in it. After five years, I'm proud of it, confident it will be liked by others after they ponder it some. I'm excited about the way the hues continue to change as time goes on.

When I was growing up, one of the things that I learned from my parents was not to ask for help. There was a lot of attention paid to being independent, and to doing things without help.

Parenting a child with special needs has me facing this "rugged individualism" part of myself. I have needed to ask for things for my daughter, which I found extremely hard to do. I am not comfortable asking for help.

I remember one time when it took all the courage I could muster to ask the manager of a local hotel if I could bring my daughter to the hotel swimming pool. I wanted to help maintain and improve her muscle tone and equilibrium during our long, cold New England winters. I was expecting to have to justify my request to this man, or maybe I was fearing humiliation, but I remember feeling very vulnerable just asking. I was pleasantly surprised when the manager gave us permission to swim in the pool, and he did not even ask for any detailed explanation.

I felt such relief when he said yes, but I also wondered why I had so dreaded asking. The worst thing that could have happened was a "no" answer – so what?

Anyway, we have had an occasional swim in the indoor pool over the past four years. I will always be grateful to the hotel manager. And I will always remember the lesson that I learned that day. It's okay to ask for help. Sometimes the answer may be yes, and sometimes it may be no. But at least I will have asked. Asking for help is one of those things that I still do not look forward to doing, but through my daughter I am learning that it is okay to ask.

What has happened to our child is hurtful – it hurts us – and it hurts when people respond inappropriately to us. I have to put on a strong face for him. He is an amputee and people stare at him, and it's hurtful to him and to me as his parent. People don't realize how rude they are when it comes to kids who look or act differently.

People are constantly trying to tell me "success" stories about someone they know with Down syndrome who bags groceries. That really isn't helpful. I've consciously chosen not to think about my child's adulthood. I don't want to put any limits on him by *my* dreams. I have no idea what he'll be able to achieve, the future is open to him.

I feel like a new woman. I got away *by myself* for three and a half days. I had to struggle to keep that time from shrinking due to everyone else's needs. Why is it I think my needs are of lesser priority than those of others? (Between my upbringing and our culture in general, I know the answer to that question...)

I stayed at a friend's house for a day and a half. While she was at work, I played the piano, sipped tea, slept, and just soaked up the quiet. Then another friend (also a mom in need of a getaway) and I went to a retreat center along the ocean for two days. We talked with each other some, but she and I both knew that the purpose of our weekend was to enjoy the quiet, and to keep talking to a minimum. So we were very introspective.

Over the weekend, I really took off my "backpack" of all the

> *Sometimes you just don't have the energy to do anything extra, even if it is important. Sometimes you just have to pull back and let some things go.*
>
> *Lynn*

responsibilities I usually carry around. If I started to think of my children or my husband, I would tell myself, "No, I'm not going to focus on them this weekend. This time is for me."

I feel so refreshed from my weekend away. It was time when I did not have to take care of anybody but myself. That's probably the first time in nine years that I have had more than a few hours to focus on myself. Not special needs, not children's needs, not husband's needs, not employer's needs, not the environment's needs, and not any of the other plethora of the world's needs. It was just time to be, and not time to do.

I really need to do this more often, or else I might lose touch with my "self."

I've learned to chuckle when people tell us what a blessing Joel is, or how we've been chosen by God for this special task in life. If it's all such a blessing, why isn't everyone praying for a child with a disability?! I realize they mean well, but it sometimes sounds so absurd.

Jeremy was in the Special Olympics last Friday. It was really interesting. They had little podiums for first, second and third place, and they pushed the wheelchairs up behind them. Then they played the Olympic theme song and put the ribbons around the kids' necks. It was really interesting.

What was especially interesting for me was the boy who was racing in front of Jeremy. He was seventeen and a sophomore in high school. He had cerebral palsy (CP). I could feel that he was listening to everything that I was saying to Jeremy and the people around Jeremy. So I turned to talk to him, and he was just the most interesting young man. I said, "How's high school? What's it like?" He said, "Well, the kids got used to me this year, finally. It took a year for them to get used to me being there." He was very articulate, and I enjoyed the opportunity to meet him and talk to him. I don't get that insight from Jeremy because Jeremy can't really tell me what it's like for him. It was really interesting to talk with someone who could tell me what it was like.

What do we do with our anger? That's my problem. I need enough anger to motivate me to keep doing this work, because sometimes that helps, but

> *You can't always show your bruises when you are out there acting as a professional or an advocate, you don't have permission to do this. You need to present yourself well to be successful.*
>
> *Kathy*

I'm reaching a point where I'm going to be ineffective in a Parent Evaluation Team (PET) meeting because I am so frustrated with people.

It's like I get so angry I start to cry. I don't want to cry. People can just dismiss you when you cry. They think, "Oh, she's over emotional," they don't hear what you're saying when they're diverted with tears. But that's what I do when I get really angry, I cry. Then I get mad at myself; but instead of expressing my anger, I cry. That doesn't feel very good, but I struggle with what to do about it, when I'm getting to the point that I'm feeling really angry and frustrated. I hate that.

Before Jess' last PET meeting, I was feeling very vulnerable. I didn't want to cry in front of the group, so I shared my feelings and tears with a support group that I belong to (not a group specifically for issues of disabilities) the day before the PET meeting. My vulnerability wasn't gone, but it took a little pressure off. I then went to the meeting the next day and did not feel close to tears. The day after the meeting, I shared some more tears with a close friend, which helped complete this cycle.

I was happy that I wasn't forcing myself *not* to cry in that PET meeting, because I'd had enough of a release ahead of time so I could make it through the meeting without crying. I struggle with the same issue, because when I get mad I cry, and I also think that I am dismissed as being an emotionally reactive mother. I too struggle with anger that comes out in tears.

Yesterday my husband became emotional at my daughter's PET meeting. I think he was feeling helpless (I know I was) about how one teacher was stonewalling our daughter's mainstreaming

For me, it's running into brick wall after brick wall, being beaten down time after time. You eventually come to the realization that the only one who can change what you are running up against is you, that no one else is going to do it. Even though I'm not qualified, I've got to make myself qualified and do it.

Renée

needs. So his eyes welled up and his voice cracked, and then he stopped to regain his composure. The group was awkwardly speechless, but it sure did get their attention.

It's kind of a funny thing. If a mother shows tears at these PET meetings, it is a sign of weakness, and she is just being another hysterical, over-emotional mother. But it really did get their attention for a man to be emotional about his child's needs. I think they would have been more comfortable or used to seeing the father angry. I think that it's more unusual for them to see a father's pain in tears, rather than in anger.

My husband has just become aware of the issues. That sounds strange; we have a six-year-old daughter who is nonverbal, and he's just now starting to get it. It's as if his timetable is five-and-a-half years behind mine, in terms of what I started dealing with when Jess was six months old. He's recognizing that, "Gee, where have I been for five years?" It's a couple issue: the timetable, the style. There is a vast difference in the burden on the marriage when the man doesn't get it, or when the timetables are just so disparate. He's been moved to tears three different times this month in different groups talking about Jess' disability. He's just now tapping into the vulnerability that this stuff brings up. It's almost amazing that there is such a difference in dealing with this. It's a family issue, but it's a couples issue too.

Our husbands are the people on whom we are incredibly reliant to be our partners in a situation that is beyond us, in which I have no skills, no training, I have nothing here. And if I'm going to be left alone holding this incredible bag, they're going to have to know that there is going to be some resentment. It isn't just a feminist-mother, or a hysterical-mother issue. This is about the very nature of partnership and commitment and promise, and it's broken, it's broken in a lot of ways. I don't hear my other friends with "normal" kids talking about these kinds of broken promises. And I go around saying, "Is this normal?" It isn't. It's because of the very nature of having a kid with a disability.

Jeremy is absolutely a tyrant, hard to live with. When he's home, he is completely bored, he doesn't focus. It's just hard; he's a tyrant. We're going to another geneticist at the end of this month. That will be interesting. We just keep kind of making the rounds every so often. We keep pursuing it; although no one has any answers for us, we're still taking steps to try to understand him. I'm at the point where I don't expect any great answer, but I think it's very helpful for Jeremy.

When my daughter, who was five at the time, got her first portable speech computer, it was quite a big day. We knew that the key to success with this computer involved using it in ways where my daughter could feel empowered by it. So we decided that a family trip to McDonald's would be a great motivator for my daughter to try out her speech computer.

Jessica was very excited about taking her computer to McDonald's to place her first order all by herself. Our family was very excited about it, until we pulled into the parking lot. My son sort of fidgeted, and looked at a loss for words. We asked him if the computer bothered him. He said, "The computer doesn't bother me. It's really neat. It's just that...it's...different."

He then asked if he could sit with his Dad while I went to the counter to help my daughter with the "stage fright" of placing her first order. He hung back at first, then made his way to the counter as he saw that his sister was being treated very respectfully, and not as a pariah, at the counter. It was fine for my husband and me to give our son some time and space to feel comfortable with his sister's difference in this public situation.

There was something about that experience that still is very clear to me. On that day, I was acutely aware of how vulnerable my son is at times. His sister's disability most definitely affects his life. I don't want to minimize the impact that her disability has on him. I want to honor the vulnerability and pain that he will face over time due to his sister's difference.

One of the most difficult aspects of parenting a child with special needs is the feeling of isolation that many of us experience. Many times, family and friends, not knowing what to say or do, will avoid conversation regarding the child, or even avoid the parents altogether. Adding to this already difficult

> *When I read an article or a book about someone in similar circumstances, I feel validated.*
>
> — Jennie

situation, are the divergent coping strategies that husbands and wives embrace.

My own experience of parenting a child with autism has been more challenging because my husband and I have often found ourselves in different places regarding acceptance. Since I was the primary caregiver for our son, it was natural that I should take the initiative in getting assessments and a diagnosis when we became concerned about Asher's development. I asked my husband to come with me to hear the diagnosis after a series of interviews and observations, because I was petrified that my son's aloofness, lack of communication skills, and constant screaming was somehow my fault. When we received the diagnosis of pervasive developmental disorder with autistic characteristics, we were both relieved. It wasn't our fault, it had a name, we could identify some immediate steps to take.

But from that point on, our courses began to diverge. My husband rarely wanted to discuss Asher or his progress. He seemed to find my constant focus on Asher tedious and tiresome. I admit to being obsessed. I felt then, and continue to feel, that the quality of my son's life is largely dependent upon the care, education, and advocacy he receives each day as a result of my efforts. Of course, this is true for all children; parents bear an immense responsibility to nurture, educate, and otherwise prepare them for their future lives as adults. This responsibility is shared by extended family, neighbors, friends, schools, religious institutions, and so on. For the child with special needs, however, it isn't as clear how the typical family supports should or can work. The parent becomes the mediator for the child; constantly explaining, clarifying, defining, requesting, apologizing, and attempting to adapt, modify, or reorder a system designed to meet the needs of the "average" child and family. It is exhausting work, in which one parent, typically the mother, becomes immersed.

After Asher's diagnosis, I became almost totally focused on his needs and the needs of his six-month-old brother. I made myself an expert on autism, and worked through the grieving process with the social worker at the therapeutic nursery where Asher was enrolled. My husband did not have the benefit of this service, because he was busy struggling to sup-

Intrinsically, men and women deal with this very differently.

Sue

port his family as a carpenter during the recession of the early '80's. As I became ever more immersed in my caregiver role, he became more emotionally distant, spent less time at home, and seemed to me to be less in touch with the needs of his son and particularly of me.

Although I can now see how my response to this crisis situation contributed to my husband's withdrawal and alienation, at the time I felt very angry and frustrated at his apparent lack of caring. I felt lonely and emotionally abandoned at the time I needed my husband's support the most.

My husband seemed to stay "stuck" in the denial phase for a long time. (We have since discussed how frequently denial is used as a coping device in his family of origin.) One incident, which occurred when our son was nine years old (six years after his diagnosis) was particularly telling.

My husband decided to sign Asher up for the town baseball team. This was obviously very important to him. The "good father" tape playing in his head apparently included a sermon on encouraging athletic ability and sportsmanship. Additionally, he had enjoyed baseball as a child and wanted his own children to benefit from this experience. Asher was too old for the T-ball team, so that left only one alternative as my husband saw it – the baseball team.

I was absolutely shocked that he would even consider such a thing. I tried to explain to my husband that Asher did not possess the skills necessary to play baseball. He could not throw a ball with accuracy. He was playing "catch the beach ball" in his occupational therapy class. With his attention problems, it seemed unlikely that he could focus his attention on the game. His almost total lack of social skills would most certainly interfere with his ability to work as part of a team. I was very concerned that he would either get hurt physically, or be taunted and suffer emotional abuse at the hands of his teammates.

My husband, however, was totally convinced that Asher just needed some practice to bring him "up to speed," and that I was being overprotective. We argued about this for several days, me restating my fears and trying to explain logically why Asher was not prepared to be successful in the baseball arena, my husband digging in his heels and insisting that Asher deserved a chance. I offered to call the coach of the T-ball team and ask whether Asher could play

> *You have to be knocked down several times to be able to stand up.*
>
> *Pat*

with them, even though he was over the age limit. (He is in the fifth percentile for height and below the chart for weight.) This too was unacceptable to my husband.

Eventually, Brian suggested that he could volunteer as a coach so that he would always be present to help keep Asher focussed and facilitate his participation as a team player. Although I continued to be concerned about Asher's safety, I relented. Arguing was accomplishing nothing; and it occurred to me that this might just be a valuable experience for Brian, if not for Asher. At least it would bring the two of them together in a way that wasn't happening at that time and give me a much-needed respite.

> *I think there is a big difference between accepting things and still trying to change them. I can accept things, but if I had the choice, I'd still change them.*
>
> *Lynn*

I didn't go to the first practice. When they returned home, I asked Brian how it went. He told me that Asher almost got hit by a hard ball because he was "spacing out" in the outfield. Brian was obviously shaken and shared with me how anxious the whole experience had made him. He decided that would be Asher's first and *last* practice on the baseball team, but he did want me to follow up with the T-ball coach, who was very understanding and welcomed Asher to the team.

Experiences such as this one are very tough on couples. I felt exasperated at my husband for being so out of touch with his son, for questioning my "expert" opinion, and for challenging my motivation. My husband was irritated with me for not understanding the symbolic nature of the baseball experience, not honoring his need to grieve at that time, and, I suppose, for attempting to deprive him of a bonding opportunity with our son. Both of us felt misunderstood and very alone at a time when we clearly needed each other's support.

Healing...

The process of healing can be different for each person. It can include the notion of resilience: being knocked down several times, but getting back up each time; or simply putting one foot in front of the other each day, facing the neverending series of challenges, and accepting this reality. The mothers in these families agree that, just as a growing child never stops changing, healing is not a single point they reach, but an ongoing process of development, with setbacks as well as successes. They clarify that recognizing the growth and focusing on the successes help to move the process of healing forward.

The mothers' stories of healing share this process and illustrate the various levels or places different parents can be in the process.

I remember when Joel was first born, my whole life seemed shrouded in a fog of "Down syndrome." Every thought, every movement, every dream was weighted down under this horrible pressure and gloom. Six years later, "Down's syndrome" seldom enters my thoughts. Joel is just one of my children, one of my treasures. Just like his brother and sister, he brings some frustration, sadness, and anger, but mostly joy and an incredible amount of pride. I'm so thankful for these three "gifts," in all their variety and uniqueness!

My daughter will be seven years old in a few weeks. I love her so dearly that sweet tears often come to my eyes when I think of how wonderful she is. But tonight, I have sad tears in my eyes. They are familiar tears. They are my grief tears.

We invited a little girl my daughter's age to come over and play today. It takes a lot of time and energy for me to keep playtime going, because kids start

Our other two children have learned an incredible amount of tolerance through living with Joel. I watch their friends' impatience with him and know that we'll all be better people from this experience...

> *Think of the implications for society, if we could all learn to be more accepting of diversity!*
>
> *Lynn*

to get bored with a playmate who cannot talk, unless I keep the playtime moving along. My daughter's friend could talk, and was "normal" in all the "normal" ways. Tonight I am crying because I am angry and sad about my daughter's disability. I grieve for a discussion with my daughter. I grieve for all the things that "normal" little girls can do with ease, that my daughter has to struggle to achieve, if she can achieve them at all. To heck with sign language, speech computers, therapies, special education, mainstreaming, and the neverending advocacy. Tonight, I grieve for the "normal" daughter that our daughter is not.

Yet, while I grieve, I also hold deep love and joy for Jessica, knowing that she is perfect just the way she is. It is such a paradox. I am finally learning to embrace this paradox of joy and grief that I will always hold, rather than telling myself that I shouldn't feel this way. It's just the way it is. But tonight I will cry my sad tears. Then tomorrow, I'll continue on.

This grieving process, the loss, is a thing that I've dealt with. I dealt with the loss of Laura being disabled, the loss of a perfect child. I dealt with that. I remember it. I remember thinking about the wedding gown and college and crying about all of that.

What I live with every day is different than that. This isn't the grieving of the loss of my imaginary daughter. This is the sadness that goes with confronting situations moment to moment in which I cannot be effective no matter how hard I try.

The love of this child is not separate from the sadness. I'm too often in situations with people where someone says, "Oh, this is depressing, let's not talk about it anymore." That is a dismissal of everything that is also wonderful about this child. It is a dismissal.

In this awfulness is my love for this child, the glory. The gloriousness of my love for this child. It's healing. I want more of her. I want to do and be more for her. Love her more, be there for her more. It isn't separate from the sadness of her disability. It is joyful pain and it is healing.

When I first got to the point of accepting Joel for who he was, I used to think that I wouldn't change a thing about him. I want him just the way he is. I love him desperately. But that's unrealistic, because if someone walked up to me tomorrow and said, "I'll get rid of this disability for you," I'd take it.

I am a very private person. I am not one to share my tears easily with others. But I am finding that I *need* to share my sadness and anger with others, those who understand feelings about parenting a child with special needs.

I want these feelings to come out in a safe place with people who will honor my feelings, rather than in a meeting with people who might then dismiss me as being an "emotionally fraught" person. It helps me to unload these heavier feelings, so I can then have the energy to continue on.

Sometimes I wonder; if Jesse were a "normal" child, would we appreciate as much, all of the little steps? I feel sad that she has to work so hard to do what comes naturally to other children, but I also wonder if I would appreciate it as much, if things came to her more easily. *Because* she has special needs, we can stop and be so happy in the midst of what is also so painful, so sorrowful. We don't take it for granted. We are there noticing the little steps that are big. That's the joy of it, and the sorrow. It's bittersweet.

J.B.'s okay just as he is. We need to look into the future, but we are not ready for that step yet.

I work hard to keep an open path of communication with all of J.B.'s teachers and doctors. It's for his benefit. He's a wonderful child, who unfortunately is trapped with a mind that is three to four years delayed. J.B. *will* survive. He has survived many challenges and will continue to do so. He's a child of wonder; we never know what he'll do next.

Because of J.B., I strive to learn all I can about disabilities, and I advocate for other children. The next disabled child you see could be your own.

My parents were here on my birthday. My father never helps in the kitchen. He never goes into the kitchen to cook unless it's to make garlic soup, his

> *Whenever I think I know what Jessica is capable of, or what her limits are, she bursts past them. So I am learning to let her show me what she can do.*
>
> *Marti*

specialty. However, on my birthday, Dad was in the kitchen helping Jess make the frosting for my cake. He helped her hold the mixer down in the frosting, so we wouldn't end up with frosting all over the walls from Jess lifting it up and down. Both of their hands were on the mixer, and I got a picture of it. It was heartwarming to see Dad connect with Jess at her level of interest.

I remember being eight or nine and wanting to visit Paris, France. It seemed like the very center of the world, so sophisticated and grown-up. I wanted to grow up and be an artist or a writer and have adventures.

I wanted to create beautiful and unusual things.

At ten I planned my life. I had big dreams. First I would venture off to the mountains of Peru. I would live among the native people and try on another culture like others try on new clothes.

Somewhere along the line my plans changed. I exchanged my dreams for a husband and children. I had two daughters, bright and pretty, and a handsome brown-eyed son.

I gave up Paris and Peru.

But I have been able to experience a different culture. And I have made things both beautiful and unusual.

Somehow I gave birth to a son from the land of "Autism." A native. He acts as a representative, an ambassador of sorts.

The American Heritage Dictionary identifies an ambassador as an authorized messenger. Isaac performs his duties beautifully. He has all the cultural nuances that people of "Autism" are famous for. He knows that Autism etiquette demands that you never quite look your companion in the eye; that you be unpredictable but demand predictability; and that you never be the first one to say hello.

Living with an ambassador requires diplomacy, true effort to understand differences and be open-minded.

"Take life one day at a time" has taken on new meaning for me in the past six years. I can't worry about tomorrow; I need to enjoy and savor every moment of today!

Lynn

That makes me an ambassador of "Normal." To the best of my ability I try to show Isaac the whys and hows of my life and culture. In return he tries to share his knowledge of his culture with me. But Isaac's everyday behavior, so different from that of "Normal," is often puzzling and seemingly bizarre. Like many foreigners he stumbles over our difficult language. He often repeats words in an effort to make sense of our syntax. Many times he uses phrases to stand for a variety of meanings in order to communicate. More often than not he is confused by our table manners and does not understand why we sit to eat, or why he must use utensils. In his country the majority seem to prefer finger foods.

Like many people of dissimilar backgrounds who unexpectedly find themselves flung together, we have our battles. I want him to respect my ways, to compromise. We experience the stress and tension of frequent misunderstandings.

We do our best to communicate. I offer walks and bicycle riding, reading and swimming. He offers jumping, giggling and squinting. Isaac has taught me that beauty truly is in the eye of the beholder. I now see signs and logos differently. I now point out postal logos and metal objects and electric generators to him.

Dining out is passé. Intimate in-home dining is the "Autistic" thing to do, although McDonald's is acceptable.

I have had to rethink many of my Normal practices and make a decision about converting or staying true to my beliefs. I also feel that, as a good host it is important to impart some of our teachings.

Many of Isaac's people participate in activities previously unknown to you or I. They have introduced creative new hobbies such as lint collecting, hand flapping, string twirling and pace walking, which is similar to race walking but with an extremely limited distance. Physical activities such as running, jumping and bouncing are all very popular. Dancing is typically seen as a solitary art. The majority of people of Autism tend to be introverted and not very verbal. Many do not speak at all. Marriages and children are very rare, but not completely unheard of. Like people of all races and creeds, there are the few who live outside the mainstream and may pursue relationships and choose to procreate. They are the minority.

My native, who is still very young, is more typical. He prefers solitary dancing and pace walking without conversation. He likes mailboxes and can openers as well as Pepsi and chips and riding in cars.

I'm learning to be more honest and open about my feelings when I'm not okay or together. Then I feel energized by putting it out there.

Marti

I have had some influence. But I do not think he will marry or have children. He is totally dedicated to his mission. He is here to teach and to share his message.

His message is one of understanding and acceptance. So I will continue to interpret and try to understand. Perhaps one day the people of "Normal" and the people of "Autism" will learn to live together without conflict or difficulty. We can work together and hope.

I call Joel my "Goodwill Ambassador." He absolutely loves saying "hi" and "bye" to everyone he sees. I can't tell you how often I've seen people, who are grumpily shuffling through their daily activity, suddenly brighten and break into a grin when they see his smiling face. He really does bring a lot of sunshine into our lives.

For a 22-hour period of time, I thought I had cancer. I discovered a suspicious-looking something, and immediately scheduled a doctor's visit for the next day. During the wait – the longest 22 hours I've experienced in quite some time – I went through the "Why me?" questions, and decided I needed to turn some things around.

I wondered if having cancer was my way of copping out on the pain that I experience in life: the pain of parenting a child with special needs, of working out marital issues, of searching for more meaningful work than my current job, of dealing with the educational system, etc., etc.

My thoughts then turned to my children. My older child, my son, would certainly miss me, but I knew that life would go on for him. Then I considered my daughter and her special needs. I panicked. Yes, I felt pain because of Jess' special needs. I also felt great joy at the richness that her disability has brought to my life. But how would my husband be able to work, parent, and put

Turning the anger that could go inward and become depression, turning it outward to make change, can be energizing.

Marti

energy into advocating for Jess' needs? Her needs and advocacy require a lot of time, as well as physical and emotional energy. I had a hard time imagining how my work for and with Jess could be replaced. My love for my daughter has given me the strength to endure the pain of dealing with her disability. Would someone other than my husband and myself be able to love her to the extent needed to overcome the pain in dealing with her disability? I felt scared thinking about it.

Well, to make a long story short, my suspicious something was not cancer. I feel so grateful, in retrospect, for that scary day of introspection. I came to realize that even though there is pain in my life, the rewards far outweigh the pain. And I need not fear what the future holds for my daughter with her special needs, because today is really all we have. If I worry about the future, I lose the preciousness of this very moment. Thank you, God, that I am still here to feel both the joy *and* the pain of life.

I often say this serenity prayer to myself:

> "God, grant me serenity, to accept the things I cannot change" (my daughter's disability, my husband's different timetable, professionals' resistance, and/or others' attitudes toward my daughter or our family, etc.),
>
> "...courage to change the things I can..." (my attitudes, thoughts, feelings, and plan of action to advocate for my daughter's and other disabled children's rights and needs),
>
> "...and wisdom to know the difference." (through talking things over with others who understand disability issues, helping me to get clearer on knowing the difference)

I find strength and healing in these thoughts.

Marti

Afterword...

I am always struck by how little we, as people and certainly as professionals, really see what lies right in front of us. On only a few occasions are we helped to recognize what might be around us; street signs, for example, are wonderful at commanding our attention, especially those that warn of sharp curves ahead. Or, when we visit a foreign country, there are images everywhere that force us to recognize that things might be different from what we would expect: cars driving on the "other" side of the street, directional signs with symbols unknown to us, languages spoken where we recognize only a few words or sounds, customs that appear unusual. As travelers with passports, we expect such differences, even welcome them. Moreover, we have undertaken the travel, oftentimes, to get away from the familiar, to "see all there is to see." It is exciting and fun. We are ready to see.

When a family comes into my office for a visit, they hope that I, as a clinical social worker, will help them to "see" the problems. I expect to be able to relate to them, to be open to what they want to tell me. When I enter into a journey with a parent or family, I know I need to remain aware of the likelihood of encountering hidden differences, unknown territory, uncharted waters. As I have learned over the years, this is what always happens when a mother and father come to me with issues relating to the care of a child with special needs. I enter another culture of sorts: I cannot assume that I will understand the emotional terrain of their lives. If I do not remain acutely aware of this, more often than not I am going to be less helpful to this family than I would like, or have the capacity, to be.

In this heartfelt book, courageous, well-traveled mothers have shared their journeys through life with children having various special needs. They speak a common language, born of anxiety, uncertainty, perseverance, and commitment. They express feelings of sorrow and joy that emanate from common passions and love for their children. They bring to us a keen sense of the strength of the human spirit, their spirits having developed in ways often very different from the lessons learned by parents of healthy children. I am humbled by all of their stories. How hard it is to have a child with special needs; what barriers these parents must overcome; the enormous amount of energy it requires! It's a constant balancing act.

If we as professionals, fellow parents and travelers can keep our eyes and hearts open, and follow many of the suggestions offered by the writers of these stories, we can, with these families, discover and master new territories from a position of combined strength.

It is my hope that parents and professionals can do more to share stories with one another, thereby helping to move steadily towards greater partnerships in today's challenged health care system. This book is an important step in this direction.

Susan Partridge
Project PIP Staff

About the Authors...

Pat Bowman and her husband, Phil, have three children – Jennifer, Joshua and Joel – and live in Gorham, Maine. Pat is a total brain injury (TBI) survivor. Her son Joel (called J.B. in these stories) has a learning disability of attention deficit and hyperactivity (ADHD) with a seizure disorder. Pat and her son understand each other's deficits better than anyone else. They are each other's strongest allies.

Pat and Joel hope to heal the heartaches their conditions have caused. They also hope the rejection they feel from peers and friends will lessen over time. Pat and Joel feel that everyone has needs; the only difference is the type of needs each of us has. We are in the end, however, just people.

Walter and *Marti Grady* live in Topsham, Maine and are continually faced with "interesting" challenges from their children Ryan, age 10 and Jessica, age 7.

Ryan wants to be a herpetologist when he grows up and is campaigning heavily for a pet boa constrictor.

Jessica's learning challenges and oral apraxia (nonverbalness due to motor speech deficit) do not stop her from communicating her needs and wants through use of body language, sign language and a speech computer. Like many other girls her age, her latest desire is her *very own* horse. Dream on children....

Martie Kendrick, a child care-related services coordinator, lives with her husband Brian, a construction supervisor, and two sons: fourteen-year-old Asher and twelve-year-old Zachary. Asher has autism, pervasive developmental delay, dyslexia, Tourette syndrome, developmental dyspraxia, Asperger's syndrome – diagnoses ad nauseam. Zachary is "terminally normal."

The Kendricks live in the small village of Bar Mills in southern Maine. They enjoy hiking, going to the beach and playing with Spot and Elmo, their dog and cat. Asher collects car brochures, Zach "fixes" everything (broken or not), and Martie and Brian's fondest wish is for eight full hours of uninterrupted sleep.

Jennie Ladew-Duncan and her husband Bill live outside of Chicago, Illinois, transplanted from Portland, Maine. By day Jennie is a wife and mother of three, as well as an unrecognized speech therapist, occupational therapist, psychologist and teacher. At night she is a writer/artist.

Jennie home-schools their two daughters, Beth, twelve and a half and Sarah, eight and a half. Once in a blue moon, Jennie and Bill try to pretend they are a "normal" couple. But more often than not, one or both of them are running after six-year-old Isaac, who has "incurable energy," otherwise known as autism.

Sue Mentzer lives in Portland, Maine with her husband Ray and their children Matthew and Jeremy.

Matthew is an honor roll student who loves baseball and all other sports. He has attention deficit hyperactivity disorder, a learning disability, and is gifted and talented.

Jeremy was born prematurely, diagnosed with cancer at six months, had a below-the-knee amputation, one year of chemotherapy and nine years later is cancer-free. He walks with the aid of a prosthesis and a brace. He faces the daily challenge of developmental delays that are believed to be part of an as-yet undiagnosed syndrome. Jeremy loves school, and collects pencils and toy school buses.

Renée Newman and her family live in Portland, Maine. Theirs is a "typical" family of four: mom, dad, Elyse (nine years old) and Robby (four years old). The fact that both Elyse and Robby were born very prematurely with major medical complications has, says Renée, "Changed our lives forever. It has enriched and strengthened our family bond!"

Ruth Pease lives with her family in rural Maine. Her oldest son, now four years old, shows no signs of his prematurity and low birth weight that kept him in the NICU for his first weeks of life. Ruth hopes to continue to be involved with the NICU where he began, by offering support to other parents of premature babies.

Lynn Spadinger lives in Cape Elizabeth, Maine with her husband Mike, children Gretchen, Alex and Joel, and their chocolate Lab, Emma.

Although Joel's Down syndrome has brought special challenges to their family, it has also brought much joy and closeness. Their favorite activities are hiking, swimming, biking, skiing, and just being together.

Kathy Son lives in Kennebunk, Maine with her husband Marc and their two children, Dustin, who is ten years old, and Laura, who is eight and a half years old. Laura has cerebral palsy and a variety of learning, emotional and social challenges. The Sons are deeply grateful to all professionals with educated hearts.

About Project PIP...

The Parents in Partnership (PIP) Project was conducted by the Edmund S. Muskie Institute of Public Affairs at the University of Southern Maine (USM) in Portland, funded by a grant from the U.S. Maternal and Child Health Bureau.

Project PIP was designed to assist in the development of a continuum of services to parents of young children with special needs. This was accomplished in part by developing multiple products to help parents and professionals form more effective partnerships through better communication skills, and to heighten professional awareness of the strengths and concerns of families who have children with special needs.

This book, a collection of stories from mothers of children with special needs, serves as a supportive product for parents. A videotape entitled *Every Child a Treasure* is aimed at increasing professionals' awareness and understanding of families in these challenging circumstances. PIP training videotapes for professionals include:

- *Parent-Professional Communication: Problem Versus Opportunity*
- *An Inside Look: Helping Parents Receive a Difficult Diagnosis*

✋ *Parenting a Child with Special Needs: A Trilogy*
  1. *Learning a Diagnosis for the First Time*
  2. *Coping with a Child with Special Needs*
  3. *Fathering a Child with Special Needs*

Susan E. Partridge, L.C.S.W., Ph.D., acted as Principal Investigator for the Project. Susan is a Research Associate at the Muskie Institute and also a private practice clinician in Portland working with families and young children.

John Hornstein, M.Ed., acted as Project Director and is also a Research Associate at the Muskie Institute. John additionally teaches Human Development at USM, and is currently pursuing his Doctorate at Harvard University.

Susan B. Soule, L.C.S.W., was Project Coordinator. Susan is a Research Associate at the Muskie Institute and a clinical social worker in the NICU at Maine Medical Center in Portland.

Jayne D.B. Marsh, M.S.N., M.P.A., was a Consultant on the Project and served as editor for this collection of stories. Jayne is a Research Associate at the Muskie Institute and teaches a parenting class through the USM Continuing Education Department.

Deborah Devine, Psy.D., was a Consultant on the Project and is a Research Associate at the Muskie Institute. Debi is also a private practice clinician working with families and young children.

Carol Boggis, M.S., is a Consulting Editor and owner of *cjb productions* in Portland. She has edited numerous Muskie Institute publications about family issues.

Key Words...

ADD	Attention Deficit Disorder
ADHD	Attention Deficit Hyperactivity Disorder
CP	Cerebral Palsy
IEP	Individualized Education Program
ICU	Intensive Care Unit
LD	Learning Disability
NICU	Neonatal Intensive Care Unit
OT	Occupational Therapist
PET	Parent Evaluation Team
PDD	Pervasive Developmental Disorder
PT	Physical Therapist
ST	Speech Therapist
TPN	Total Parental Nutrition